ISBN 0-8373-0416-4

C-416   CAREER EXAMINATION SERIES

This is your
PASSBOOK® for...

Executive Director of Youth Bureau

Test Preparation Study Guide

Questions & Answers

NATIONAL LEARNING CORPORATION

(516) 921-8888
(800) 645-6337
FAX: (516) 921-8743
www.passbooks.com
sales @ passbooks.com
info @ passbooks.com

PRINTED IN THE UNITED STATES OF AMERICA

PASSBOOK®
NOTICE

This book is SOLELY intended for, is sold ONLY to, and its use is RESTRICTED to *individual*, bona fide applicants or candidates who qualify by virtue of having seriously filed applications for appropriate license, certificate, professional and/or promotional advancement, higher school matriculation, scholarship, or other legitimate requirements of educational and/or governmental authorities.

This book is NOT intended for use, class instruction, tutoring, training, duplication, copying, reprinting, excerption, or adaptation, etc., by:

(1) Other publishers

(2) Proprietors and/or Instructors of "Coaching" and/or Preparatory Courses

(3) Personnel and/or Training Divisions of commercial, industrial, and governmental organizations

(4) Schools, colleges, or universities and/or their departments and staffs, including teachers and other personnel

(5) Testing Agencies or Bureaus

(6) Study groups which seek by the purchase of a single volume to copy and/or duplicate and/or adapt this material for use by the group as a whole without having purchased individual volumes for each of the members of the group

(7) Et al.

Such persons would be in violation of appropriate Federal and State statutes.

PROVISION OF LICENSING AGREEMENTS. — Recognized educational commercial, industrial, and governmental institutions and organizations, and others legitimately engaged in educational pursuits, including training, testing, and measurement activities, may address a request for a licensing agreement to the copyright owners, who will determine whether, and under what conditions, including fees and charges, the materials in this book may be used by them. In other words, a licensing facility exists for the legitimate use of the material in this book on other than an individual basis. However, it is asseverated and affirmed here that the material in this book *CANNOT* be used without the receipt of the express permission of such a licensing agreement from the Publishers.

NATIONAL LEARNING CORPORATION
212 Michael Drive
Syosset, New York 11791

Inquiries re licensing agreements should be addressed to:
The President
National Learning Corporation
212 Michael Drive
Syosset, New York 11791

PASSBOOK SERIES®

THE *PASSBOOK SERIES®* has been created to prepare applicants and candidates for the ultimate academic battlefield—the examination room.

At some time in our lives, each and every one of us may be required to take an examination—for validation, matriculation, admission, qualification, registration, certification, or licensure.

Based on the assumption that every applicant or candidate has met the basic formal educational standards, has taken the required number of courses, and read the necessary texts, the *PASSBOOK SERIES®* furnishes the one special preparation which may assure passing with confidence, instead of failing with insecurity. Examination questions—together with answers—are furnished as the basic vehicle for study so that the mysteries of the examination and its compounding difficulties may be eliminated or diminished by a sure method.

This book is meant to help you pass your examination provided that you qualify and are serious in your objective.

The entire field is reviewed through the huge store of content information which is succinctly presented through a provocative and challenging approach—the question-and-answer method.

A climate of success is established by furnishing the correct answers at the end of each test.

You soon learn to recognize types of questions, forms of questions, and patterns of questioning. You may even begin to anticipate expected outcomes.

You perceive that many questions are repeated or adapted so that you gain acute insights, which may enable you to score many sure points.

You learn how to confront new questions, or types of questions, and to attack them confidently and work out the correct answers.

You note objectives and emphases, and recognize pitfalls and dangers, so that you may make positive educational adjustments.

Moreover, you are kept fully informed in relation to new concepts, methods, practices, and directions in the field.

You discover that you are actually taking the examination all the time: you are preparing for the examination by "taking" an examination, not by reading extraneous and/or supererogatory textbooks.

In short, this PASSBOOK®, used directedly, should be an important factor in helping you to pass your test.

EXECUTIVE DIRECTOR OF YOUTH BUREAU

DUTIES

An employee in this class plans, designs and administers the activities of a municipal Youth Bureau. The incumbent is responsible for the overall administration of the Youth Bureau in providing technical assistance to community agencies, developing training programs for counselors and coordinating programs with state, federal and local agencies. The incumbent exercises a considerable amount of independent judgment and initiative. Supervision is exercised over a professional and clerical staff, and is received from an administrative supervisor through conferences and written reports. Does related work as required.

SCOPE OF THE EXAMINATION

The written test will cover knowledge, skills, and/or abilities in such areas as:

1. Administering and coordinating youth programs;
2. Educating and interacting with the public;
3. Preparing written material;
4. Supervision;
5. Working with youth.

HOW TO TAKE A TEST

I. YOU MUST PASS AN EXAMINATION

A. WHAT EVERY CANDIDATE SHOULD KNOW

Examination applicants often ask us for help in preparing for the written test. What can I study in advance? What kinds of questions will be asked? How will the test be given? How will the papers be graded?

As an applicant for a civil service examination, you may be wondering about some of these things. Our purpose here is to suggest effective methods of advance study and to describe civil service examinations.

Your chances for success on this examination can be increased if you know how to prepare. Those "pre-examination jitters" can be reduced if you know what to expect. You can even experience an adventure in good citizenship if you know why civil service examinations are given.

B. WHY ARE CIVIL SERVICE EXAMINATIONS GIVEN?

Civil service examinations are important to you in two ways. As a citizen, you want public jobs filled by employees who know how to do their work. As a job-seeker, you want a fair chance to compete for that job on an equal footing with other candidates. The best known means of accomplishing this two-fold goal is the competitive examination.

Examinations are widely publicized throughout the nation. They may be administered for jobs in federal, state, city, municipal, town, or village governments or agencies.

Any citizen may apply, with some limitations, such as the age or residence of applicants. Your experience and education may be reviewed to see whether you meet the requirements for the particular examination. When these requirements exist, they are reasonable and are applied consistently to all applicants. Thus, a competitive examination may cause you some uneasiness now, but it is your privilege and safeguard.

C. HOW ARE CIVIL SERVICE EXAMINATIONS DEVELOPED?

Examinations are carefully written by trained technicians who are specialists in the field known as "psychological measurement," in consultation with recognized authorities in the field of work that the test will cover. These experts recommend the subject matter areas or skills to be tested; only those knowledges or skills important to your success on the job are included. The most reliable books and source materials available are used as references. Together, the experts and technicians judge the difficulty level of the questions.

Test technicians know how to phrase questions so that the problem is clearly stated. Their ethics do not permit "trick" or "catch" questions. Questions may have been tried out on sample groups, or subjected to statistical analysis, to determine their usefulness.

Written tests are often used in combination with performance tests, ratings of training and experience, and oral interviews. All of these measures combine to form the best known means of finding the right man for the right job.

II. HOW TO PASS THE WRITTEN TEST

A. *NATURE OF THE EXAMINATION*

To prepare intelligently for civil service examinations, you should know how they differ from school examinations you have taken. In school you were assigned certain definite pages to read or subjects to cover. The examination questions were quite detailed and usually emphasized memory. Civil service examinations, on the other hand, try to discover your present ability to perform the duties of a position, plus your potentiality to learn these duties. In other words, a civil service examination attempts to predict how successful you will be. Questions cover such a broad area that they cannot be as minute and detailed as school examination questions.

In the public service similar kinds of work, or positions, are grouped together in one "class." This process is known as "position-classification." All the positions in a class are paid according to the salary range for that class. One class title covers all these positions, and they are all tested by the same examination.

B. *FOUR BASIC STEPS*

1. Study the Announcement.--How, then, can you know what subjects to study? Our best answer is: "Learn as much as possible about the class of positions for which you have applied." The examination will test the knowledge, skills, and abilities needed to do the work.

Your most valuable source of information about the position you want is the official announcement of the examination. This announcement lists the training and experience qualifications. Check these standards and apply only if you come reasonably close to meeting them.

The brief description of the position in the examination announcement offers some clues to the subjects which will be tested. Think about the job itself. Review the duties in your mind. Can you perform them, or are there some in which you are rusty? Fill in the blank spots in your preparation.

Many jurisdictions preview the written test in the examination announcement by including a section called "Knowledge and Abilities Required," "Scope of Examination," or some similar heading. Here you will find out specifically what fields will be tested.

2. Review Your Own Background.-- Once you learn in general what the position is all about, and what you need to know to do the work, ask yourself which subjects you already know fairly well and which need improvement. You may wonder whether to concentrate on improving your strong areas or on building some background in your fields of weakness. When the announcement has specified "some knowledge" or "considerable knowledge," or has used adjectives such as "beginning principles of ...." or "advanced .....methods," you can get a clue as to the number and difficulty of questions to be asked in any given field. More questions, and hence broader coverage, would be included for those subjects which are more important in the work. Now weigh your strengths and weaknesses against the job requirements and prepare accordingly.

3. Determine the Level of the Position.-- Another way to tell how intensively you should prepare is to understand the level of the job for which you are applying. Is it the entering level? In other words, is this the position in which beginners in a field of work are hired? Or is it an intermediate or advanced level? Sometimes this is indicated by such words as "Junior" or "Senior" in the class title.Other jurisdictions use Roman numerals to designate the level: Clerk I,

Clerk II, for example. The word "Supervisor" sometimes appears in the title. If the level is not indicated by the title, check the description of duties. Will you be working under very close supervision, or will you have responsibility for independent decisions in this work?

4. Choose Appropriate Study Materials.-- Now that you know the subjects to be examined and the relative amount of each subject to be covered, you can choose suitable study materials. For beginning level jobs, or even advanced ones, if you have a pronounced weakness in some aspect of your training, read a modern, standard textbook in that field. Be sure it is up-to-date and has general coverage. Such books are normally available at your library, and the librarian will be glad to help you locate one. For entry level positions, questions of appropriate difficulty are chosen -- neither highly advanced questions, nor those too simple. Such questions require careful thought but not advanced training.

If the position for which you are applying is technical or advanced, you will read more advanced, specialized material. If you are already familiar with the basic principles of your field, elementary textbooks would waste your time. Concentrate on advanced textbooks and technical periodicals. Think through the concepts and review difficult problems in your field.

These are all general sources. You can get more ideas on your own initiative, following these leads. For example, training manuals and publications of the government agency which employs workers in your field can be useful, particularly for technical and professional positions. A letter or visit to the government department involved may result in more specific study suggestions, and certainly will provide you with a more definite idea of the exact nature of the position you are seeking.

III. KINDS OF TESTS

Tests are used for purposes other than measuring knowledge and ability to perform specified duties. For some positions, it is equally important to test ability to make adjustments to new situations or to profit from training. In others, basic mental abilities not dependent upon information are essential. Questions which test these things may not appear as pertinent to the duties of the position as those which test for knowledge and information. Yet they are often highly important parts of a fair examination. For very general questions, it is almost impossible to help you direct your study efforts. What we can do is to point out some of the more common of these general abilities needed in public service positions and describe some typical questions.

1. General Information

Broad, general information has been found useful for predicting job success in some kinds of work. This is tested in a variety of ways, from vocabulary lists to questions about current events. Basic background in some field of work, such as sociology or economics, may be sampled in a group of questions. Often these are principles which have become familiar to most persons through "exposure" rather than through formal training. It is difficult to advise you how to study for these questions; being alert to the world around you is our best suggestion.

2. Verbal Ability

An example of an ability needed in many positions is verbal or language ability. Verbal ability is, in brief, the ability to use and understand words. Vocabulary and grammar tests are typical measures of this ability. "Reading comprehension" or "paragraph interpretation" questions are common in many kinds of civil service tests. You are given a paragraph of written material and asked to find its central meaning.

3. Numerical Ability

Number skills can be tested by the familiar arithmetic problem, by checking paired lists of numbers to see which are alike and which are different, or by interpreting charts and graphs. In the latter test, a graph may be printed in the test booklet which you are asked to use as the basis for answering questions.

4. Observation

A popular test for law-enforcement positions is the observation test. A picture is shown to you for several minutes, then taken away. Questions about the picture test your ability to observe both details and larger elements.

5. Following Directions

In many positions in the public service, the employee must be able to carry out written instructions dependably and accurately. You may be given a chart with several columns, each column listing a variety of information. The questions require you to carry out directions involving the information given in the chart.

6. Skills and Aptitudes

Performance tests effectively measure some manual skills and aptitudes. When the skill is one in which you are trained, such as typing or shorthand, you can practice. These tests are often very much like those given in business school or high school courses. For many of the other skills and aptitudes, however, no short-time preparation can be made. Skills and abilities natural to you or that you have developed throughout your lifetime are being tested.

Many of the general questions just described provide all the data needed to answer the questions and ask you to use your reasoning ability to find the answers. Your best preparation for these tests, as well as for tests of facts and ideas, is to be at your physical and mental best. You, no doubt, have your own methods of getting into an exam-taking mood and keeping "in shape." The next section lists some ideas on this subject.

IV. KINDS OF QUESTIONS

Only rarely is the "essay" question, which you answer in narrative form, used in civil service tests. Civil service tests are usually of the short-answer type. Full instructions for answering these questions will be given to you at the examination. But in case this is your first experience with short-answer questions and separate answer sheets, here is what you need to know.

1. Multiple-Choice Questions

Most popular of the short-answer questions is the "multiple-choice" or "best-answer" question. It can be used, for example, to test for factual knowledge, ability to solve problems, or judgment in meeting situations found at work.

A multiple-choice question is normally one of three types:

(1) It can begin with an incomplete statement followed by several possible endings. You are to find the one ending which *best* completes the statement, although some of the others may not be entirely wrong.

(2) It can also be a complete statement in the form of a question which is answered by choosing one of the statements listed.

(3) It can be in the form of a problem -- again you select the best answer.

Here is an example of a multiple-choice question with a discussion which should give you some clues as to the method for choosing the right answer.

SAMPLE QUESTION:

When an employee has a complaint about his assignment, the action which will *best* help him overcome his difficulty is

  (A) to discuss his difficulty with his co-workers
  (B) to take the problem to the head of the organization
  (C) to take the problem to the person who gave him the assignment
  (D) to say nothing to anyone about his complaint

In answering this question you should study each of the choices to find which is best. Consider choice (A). Certainly an employee may discuss his complaint with fellow employees, but no change or improvement can result, and the complaint remains unsolved. Choice (B) is a poor choice since the head of the organization probably does not know what assignment you have been given, and taking your problem to him is known as "going over the head" of the supervisor. The supervisor, or person who made the assignment, is the person who can clarify it or correct any injustice. Choice (C) is, therefore, correct. To say nothing, as in choice (D), is unwise. Supervisors have an interest in knowing the problems employees are facing, and the employee is seeking a solution to his problem.

2. True-False Questions

The "true-false" or "right-wrong" form of question is sometimes used. Here a complete statement is given. Your problem is to decide whether the statement is right or wrong.

SAMPLE QUESTION:

A person-to-person long distance telephone call costs less than a station-to-station call to the same city.

This question is wrong, or "false," since person-to-person calls are more expensive.

This is not a complete list of all possible question forms, although most of the others are variations of these common types. You will always get complete directions for answering questions. Be sure you understand *how* to mark your answers -- ask questions until you do.

V. RECORDING YOUR ANSWERS

For an examination with very few applicants, you may be told to record your answers in the test booklet itself. Separate answer sheets are much more common. If this separate answer sheet is to be scored by machine -- and this is often the case -- it is highly important that you mark your answers correctly in order to get credit.

An electric test-scoring machine is often used in civil service offices because of the speed with which papers can be scored. Machine-scored answer sheets must be marked with a special pencil, which will be given to you. This pencil has a high graphite content which responds to the electrical scoring machine. As a matter of fact, stray dots may register as answers, so do not let your pencil rest on the answer sheet while you are pondering the correct answer. Also, if your pencil lead breaks or is otherwise defective, ask for another.

Since the answer sheet will be dropped in a slot in the scoring machine, be careful not to bend the corners or get the paper crumpled.

The answer sheet normally has five vertical columns of numbers, with 30 numbers to a column. These numbers correspond to the question numbers in your test booklet. After each number, going across the page, are four or five pairs of dotted lines. These short dotted lines have small letters or numbers above them. The first two pairs may also have a "T" and "F" above the letters. This indicates that the first two pairs only are to be used if the questions are of the true-false type. If the questions are multiple-choice, disregard this "T" and "F" completely, and pay attention only to the small number or letters.

Answer your questions in the manner of the sample that follows. Proceed in the sequential steps outlined below.

Assume that you are answering question 32, which is:

   32. The largest city in the United States is:

       A. Washington, D.C.   B. New York City   C. Chicago

       D. Detroit   E. San Francisco

1. Choose the answer you think is best.

   New York City is the largest, so choice B is correct.

2. Find the row of dotted lines numbered the same as the question you are answering.

   This is question number 32, so find row number 32.

3. Find the pair of dotted lines corresponding to the answer you have chosen.

   You have chosen answer B, so find the pair of dotted lines marked "B".

4. Make a solid black mark between the dotted lines.

   Go up and down two or three times with your pencil so plenty of graphite rubs off, but do not let the mark get outside or above the dots.

VI. BEFORE THE TEST

Common sense will help you find procedures to follow to get ready for an examination. Too many of us, however, overlook these sensible measures. Indeed, nervousness and fatigue have been found to be the most serious reasons why applicants fail to do their best on civil service tests. Here is a list of reminders.

1. Begin Your Preparation Early

Don't wait until the last minute to go scurrying around for books and materials or to find out what the position is all about.

2. Prepare Continuously

An hour a night for a week is better than an all-night cram session. This has been definitely established. What is more, a night a week for a month will return better dividends than crowding your study into a shorter period of time.

3. Locate the Place of the Examination

You have been sent a notice telling you when and where to report for the examination. If the location is in a different town or otherwise unfamiliar to you, it would be well to inquire the best route and learn something about the building.

4. Relax the Night Before the Test

Allow your mind to rest. Do not study at all that night. Plan some mild recreation or diversion; then go to bed early and get a good night's sleep.

5. Get Up Early Enough to Make a Leisurely Trip to the Place for the Test

Then unforeseen events, traffic snarls, unfamiliar buildings, will not upset you.

6. Dress Comfortably

A written test is not a fashion show. You will be known by number and not by name, so wear something comfortable.

7. Leave Excess Paraphernalia at Home

Shopping bags and odd bundles will get in your way. You need bring only the items mentioned in the official notice sent to you; usually everything you need is provided. Do not bring reference books to the examination. They will only confuse those last minutes and be taken away from you when in the test room.

8. Arrive Somewhat Ahead of Time

If because of transportation schedules you must get there very early, bring a newspaper or magazine to take your mind off yourself while waiting.

9. Locate the Examination Room

When you have found the proper room, you will be directed to the seat or part of the room where you will sit. Sometimes you are given a sheet of instructions to read while you are waiting. Do not fill out any forms until you are told to do so; just read them and be ready.

10. Relax and Prepare to Listen to the Instructions

11. If you have any physical problem that may keep you from doing your best, be sure to tell the test administrator. If you are sick, or in poor health, you really cannot do your best on the test. You can come back and take the test some other time.

VII. AT THE TEST

The day of the test is here and you have the test booklet in your hand. The temptation to get going is very strong. Caution! There is more to success than knowing the right answers. You must know how to identify your papers and understand variations in the type of short-answer question used in this particular examination. Follow these suggestions for maximum results from your efforts:

1. Cooperate with the Monitor

The test administrator has a duty to create a situation in which you can be as much at ease as possible. He will give instructions, tell you when to begin, check to see that you are marking your answer sheet correctly. He is not there to guard you, although he will see that your competitors do not take unfair advantage. He wants to help you do your best.

2. Listen to All Instructions

Don't jump the gun! Wait until you understand all directions. In most civil service tests you get more time than you need to answer the questions. So don't get in a hurry. Read each word of instructions until you clearly understand the meaning. Study the examples. Listen to all announcements. Follow directions. Ask questions if you do not understand what to do.

3. Identify Your Papers

Civil service examinations are usually identified by number only. You will be assigned a number; you must not put your name on your test papers. Be sure to copy your number correctly. Since more than one examination may be given, copy your exact examination title.

4. Plan Your Time

Unless you are told that a test is a "speed" or "rate-of-work" test, speed itself is not usually important. Time enough to answer all the questions will be provided. But this does not mean that you have all day. An overall time limit has been set. Divide the total time (in minutes) by the number of questions to get the approximate time you have for each question.

5. Do Not Linger Over Difficult Questions

If you come across a difficult question, mark it with a paper clip (useful to have along) and come back to it when you have been through the booklet. One caution if you do this -- be sure to skip a number on your answer sheet too. Check often to be sure that you have not lost your place and that you are marking in the row numbered the same as the question you are answering.

6. Read the Questions

Be sure you know what the question asks! Many capable people are unsuccessful because they failed to *read* the questions correctly.

7. Answer All Questions

Unless you have been instructed that a penalty will be deducted for incorrect answers, it is better to guess than to omit a question.

8. Speed Tests

It is often better *not* to guess on speed tests. It has been found that on timed tests people are tempted to spend the last few seconds before time is called in marking answers at random -- without even reading them -- in the hope of picking up a few extra points. To discourage this practice, the instructions may warn you that your score will be "corrected" for guessing. That is, a penalty will be applied. The incorrect answers will be deducted from the correct ones, or some other penalty formula will be used.

9. Review Your Answers

If you finish before time is called, go back to the questions you guessed or omitted to give further thought to them. Review other answers if you have time.

10. Return Your Test Materials

   If you are ready to leave before others have finished or time is called, take *all* your materials to the monitor and leave quietly. Never take any test material with you. The monitor can discover whose papers are not complete, and taking a test booklet may be grounds for disqualification.

VIII. EXAMINATION TECHNIQUES

   1. Read the *general* instructions carefully. These are usually printed on the first page of the examination booklet. As a rule, these instructions refer to the timing of the examination; the fact that you should not start work until the signal and must stop work at a signal, etc. If there are any *special* instructions, such as a choice of questions to be answered, make sure that you note this instruction carefully.

   2. When you are ready to start work on the examination, that is as soon as the signal has been given, read the instructions to each question booklet, underline any key words or phrases, such as *least, best, outline, describe,* and the like. In this way you will tend to answer as requested rather than discover on reviewing your paper that you *listed without describing,* that you selected the *worst* choice rather than the *best* choice, etc.

   3. If the examination is of the objective or so-called multiple-choice type, that is, each question will also give a series of possible answers: A, B, C, or D, and you are called upon to select the best answer and write the letter next to that answer on your answer paper, it is advisable to start answering each question in turn. There may be anywhere from 50 to 100 such questions in the three or four hours allotted and you can see how much time would be taken if you read through all the questions before beginning to answer any. Furthermore, if you come across a question or a group of questions which you know would be difficult to answer, it would undoubtedly affect your handling of all the other questions.

   4. If the examination is of the esssay-type and contains but a few questions, it is a moot point as to whether you should read all the questions before starting to answer any one. Of course if you are given a choice, say five out of seven and the like, then it is essential to read all the questions so you can eliminate the two which are most difficult. If, however, you are asked to answer all the questions, there may be danger in trying to answer the easiest one first because you may find that you will spend too much time on it. The best technique is to answer the first question, then proceed to the second, etc.

   5. Time your answers. Before the examination begins, write down the time it started, then add the time allowed for the examination and write down the time it must be completed, then divide the time available somewhat as follows:

   (a) If $3\frac{1}{2}$ hours are allowed, that would be 210 minutes. If you have 80 objective-type questions, that would be an average of $2\frac{1}{2}$ minutes per question. Allow yourself no more than 2 minutes per question, or a total of 160 minutes, which will permit about 50 minutes to review.

   (b) If for the time allotment of 210 minutes, there are 7 essay questions to answer, that would average about 30 minutes a question. Give yourself only 25 minutes per question so that you have about 35 minutes to review.

6. The most important instruction is *to read each question* and make sure you know what is wanted. The second most important instruction is to *time yourself properly* so that you answer every question. The third most important instruction is to *answer every question*. Guess if you have to but include something for each question. Remember that you will receive no credit for a blank and will probably receive some credit if you write something in answer to an essay question. If you guess a letter, say "B" for a multiple-choice question, you may have guessed right. If you leave a blank as the answer to a multiple-choice question, the examiners may respect your feelings but it will not add a point to your score.

7. Suggestions

   a. <u>Objective-Type Questions</u>

     (1) Examine the question booklet for proper sequence of pages and questions.

     (2) Read all instructions carefully.

     (3) Skip any question which seems too difficult; return to it after all other questions have been answered.

     (4) Apportion your time properly; do not spend too much time on any single question or group of questions.

     (5) Note and underline key words -- *all, most, fewest, least, best, worst, same, opposite.*

     (6) Pay particular attention to negatives.

     (7) Note unusual option, e.g., unduly long, short, complex, different or similar in content to the body of the question.

     (8) Observe the use of "hedging" words -- *probably, may, most likely, etc.*

     (9) Make sure that your answer is put next to the same number as the question.

     (10) Do not second-guess unless you have good reason to believe the second answer is definitely more correct.

     (11) Cross out original answer if you decide another answer is more accurate; do not erase.

     (12) Answer all questions; guess unless instructed otherwise.

     (13) Leave time for review.

   b. <u>Essay-Type Questions</u>

     (1) Read each question carefully.

     (2) Determine exactly what is wanted. Underline key words or phrases.

     (3) Decide on outline or paragraph answer.

     (4) Include many different points and elements unless asked to develop any one or two points or elements.

     (5) Show impartiality by giving pros and cons unless directed to select one side only.

     (6) Make and write down any assumptions you find necessary to answer the question.

     (7) Watch your English, grammar, punctuation, choice of words.

     (8) Time your answers; don't crowd material.

8. Answering the Essay Question

   Most essay questions can be answered by framing the specific response around several key words or ideas. Here are a few such key words or ideas:

M's: manpower, materials, methods, money, management;
P's: purpose, program, policy, plan, procedure, practice, problems, pitfalls, personnel, public relations.

a. Six Basic Steps in Handling Problems:
(1) Preliminary plan and background development
(2) Collect information, data and facts
(3) Analyze and interpret information, data and facts
(4) Analyze and develop solutions as well as make recommendations
(5) Prepare report and sell recommendations
(6) Install recommendations and follow up effectiveness

b. Pitfalls to Avoid
(1) *Taking things for granted*
A statement of the situation does not necessarily imply that each of the elements is necessarily true; for example, a complaint may be invalid and biased so that all that can be taken for granted is that a complaint has been registered.
(2) *Considering only one side of a situation*
Wherever possible, indicate several alternatives and then point out the reasons you selected the best one.
(3) *Failing to indicate follow-up*
Whenever your answer indicates action on your part, make certain that you will take proper follow-up action to see how successful your recommendations, procedures, or actions turn out to be.
(4) *Taking too long in answering any single question*
Remember to time your answers properly.

IX. AFTER THE TEST

Scoring procedures differ in detail among civil service jurisdictions although the general principles are the same. Whether the papers are hand-scored or graded by the electric scoring machine we have described, they are nearly always graded by number. That is, the person who marks the paper knows only the number -- never the name -- of the applicant. Not until all the papers have been graded will they be matched with names. If other tests, such as training and experience or oral interview ratings have been given, scores will be combined. Different parts of the examination usually have different weights. For example, the written test might count 60 percent of the final grade, and a rating of training and experience 40 percent. In many jurisdictions, veterans will have a certain number of points added to their grades.

After the final grade has been determined, the names are placed in grade order and an eligible list is established. There are various methods for resolving ties between those who get the same final grade: probably the most common is to place first the name of the person whose application was received first. Job offers are made from the eligible list in the order the names appear on it.

You will be notified of your grade and your rank order as soon as all these computations have been made. This will be done as rapidly as possible.

People who are found to meet the requirements in the announcement are called "eligibles." Their names are put on a list of eligibles. An eligible's chances of getting a job depend on how high he stands on this list and how fast agencies are filling jobs from the list.

When a job is to be filled from a list of eligibles, the agency asks for the names of people on the list of eligibles for that job.

When the civil service commission receives this request, it sends to the agency the names of the three people highest on the list. Or, if the job to be filled has specialized requirements, the office sends the agency, from the general list, the names of the top three persons who meet those requirements.

The appointing officer makes a choice from among the three people whose names were sent to him. If the selected person accepts the appointment, the names of the others are put back on the list to be considered for future openings.

That is the rule in hiring from all kinds of eligible lists, whether they are for typist, carpenter, chemist, or something else. For every vacancy, the appointing officer has his choice of any one of the top three eligibles on the list. This explains why the person whose name is on top of the list sometimes does not get an appointment when some of the persons lower on the list do. If the appointing officer chooses the No.2 or No.3 eligible, the No.1 eligible does not get a job at once, but stays on the list until he is appointed or the list is terminated.

X. HOW TO PASS THE INTERVIEW TEST

The examination for which you applied requires an oral interview test. You have already taken the written test and you are now being called for the interview test -- the final part of the formal examination.

You may think that it is not possible to prepare for an interview test and that there are no procedures to follow during an interview.

Our purpose is to point out some things you can do in advance that will help you and some good rules to follow and pitfalls to avoid while you are being interviewed.

A. WHAT IS AN INTERVIEW SUPPOSED TO TEST?

The written examination is designed to test the technical knowledge and competence of the candidate; the oral is designed to evaluate intangible qualities, not readily measured otherwise, and to establish a list showing the relative fitness of each candidate, *as measured against his competitors,* for the position sought. Scoring is not on the basis of "right" or "wrong," but on a sliding scale of values ranging from "not passable" to "outstanding." As a matter of fact, it is possible to achieve a relatively low score without a single "incorrect" answer because of evident weakness in the qualities being measured.

Occasionally, an examination may consist entirely of an oral test -- either an individual or a group oral. In such cases, information is sought concerning the technical knowledges and abilities of the candidate, since there has been no written examination for this purpose. More commonly, however, an oral test is used to supplement a written examination.

B. WHO CONDUCTS INTERVIEWS?

The composition of oral boards varies among different jurisdictions. In nearly all, a representative of the personnel department serves as chairman. One of the members of the board may be a representative of the department in which the candidate would work. In some cases, "outside experts" are used, and, frequently, a business man or some other representative of the general public is asked to serve. Labor and management or other special groups may be represented. The aim is to secure the services of experts in the appropriate field.

However the board is composed, it is a good idea (and not at all improper or unethical) to ascertain in advance of the interview who the members are and what groups they represent. When you are introduced to them, you will have some idea of their backgrounds and interests, and at least you will not stutter and stammer over their names.

C. *WHAT TO DO BEFORE THE INTERVIEW*

While knowledge about the board members is useful and takes some of the surprise element out of the interview, there is other preparation which is more substantive. It *is* possible to prepare for an oral -- in several ways:

1. Keep a Copy of Your Application and Review it Carefully Before the Interview

   This may be the only document before the oral board, and the starting point of the interview. Know what experience and education you have listed there, and the sequence and dates of it. Sometimes the board will ask *you* to review the highlights of your experience for them; you should not have to hem and haw doing it.

2. Study the Class Specification and the Examination Announcement

   Usually, the oral board has one or both of these to guide them. The qualities, characteristics, or knowledges required by the position sought are stated in these documents. They offer valuable clues as to the nature of the oral interview. For example, if the job involves supervisory responsibilities, the announcement will usually indicate that knowledge of modern supervisory methods and the qualifications of the candidate as a supervisor will be tested. If so, you can expect such questions, frequently in the form of a hypothetical situation which you are expected to solve. *Never* go into an oral without knowledge of the duties and responsibilities of the job you seek.

3. Think Through Each Qualification Required

   Try to visualize the kind of questions *you* would ask if you were a board member. How well could you answer them? Try especially to appraise your own knowledge and background in each area, *measured against the job sought,* and identify any areas in which you are weak. Be critical and realistic -- do not flatter yourself.

4. Do Some General Reading in Areas in Which You Feel You May be Weak

   For example, if the job involves supervision and your past experience has *not,* some general reading in supervisory methods and practices, particularly in the field of human relations, might be useful. *Do not* study agency procedures or detailed manuals. The oral board will be testing your understanding and capacity, *not* your memory.

5. Get a Good Night's Sleep and Watch Your General Health and Mental Attitude

   You will want a clear head at the interview. Take care of a cold or other minor ailment, and, of course, *no hangovers.*

D. WHAT TO DO THE DAY OF THE INTERVIEW

Now comes the day of the interview itself. Give yourself plenty of time to get there. Plan to arrive somewhat ahead of the scheduled time, particularly if your appointment is in the fore part of the day. If a previous candidate fails to appear, the board might be ready for you a bit early. By early afternoon an oral board is almost invariably behind schedule if there are many candidates, and you may have to wait. Take along a book or magazine to read, or your application to review. But leave any extraneous material in the waiting room when you go in for your interview. In any event, relax and compose yourself.

The matter of dress is important. The board is forming impressions about you -- from your experience, your manners, your attitudes, and from your appearance. Give your personal appearance careful attention. Dress your *best*, but not your flashiest. Choose conservative, appropriate clothing, and be sure it and you are immaculate. This is a business interview, and your appearance should indicate that you regard it as such. Besides, being well-groomed and properly dressed will help boost your confidence.

Sooner or later, someone will call your name and escort you into the interview room. *This is it*. From here on you are on your own. It is too late for any more preparation. But, remember, you asked for this opportunity to prove your fitness, and you are here because your request was granted.

E. WHAT HAPPENS WHEN YOU GO IN?

The usual sequence of events will be as follows: The clerk (who is often the board stenographer) will introduce you to the chairman of the oral board, who will introduce you to each other member of the board. Acknowledge the introductions before you sit down. Do not be surprised if you find a microphone facing you or a stenotypist sitting by. Oral interviews are usually recorded, in the event of an appeal or other review.

Usually the chairman of the board will open the interview by reviewing the highlights of your education and work experience from your application -- primarily for the benefit of the other members of the board, as well as to get the material into the record. Do not interrupt or comment unless there is an error or significant misinterpretation; if so, do not hesitate. But do not quibble about insignificant matters. Usually, also, he will ask you some question about your education, your experience, or your present job -- partly to get you started talking, to establish the interviewing "rapport." He may start the actual questioning, or turn it over to one of the other members. Frequently each member undertakes the questioning on a particular area, one in which he is perhaps most competent. So you can expect each member to participate in the examination. And because the time is limited, you may expect some rather abrupt switches in the direction the questioning takes. Do not be upset by it. Normally, a board member will not pursue a single line of questioning unless he discovers a particular strength or weakness.

After each member has participated, the chairman will usually ask whether any member has any further questions, then will ask you if you have anything you wish to add. Unless you are expecting this question, it may floor you. Or worse, it may start you off on an extended, extemporaneous speech. The board is not usually seeking more information. The question is principally to offer you a last opportunity to present further qualifications or to indicate that you have nothing to add. So, if you feel that a significant qualification or characteristic has been overlooked, it is proper to point it out in a sentence or so. Do not compliment the board on the thoroughness of their examination -- they have been sketchy, and you know it. If you wish, merely say, "No thank you, I have nothing further to add." This is a point where you can "talk yourself out" of a good impression or fail to present an important bit of information. *Remember, you close the interview yourself.*

The chairman will then say,"That is all,Mr.Smith,thank you." Do not be startled; the interview is over, and quicker than you think. Say,"Thank you and good morning," gather up your belongings and take your leave. Save your sigh of relief for the other side of the door.

F. *HOW TO PUT YOUR BEST FOOT FORWARD*

Throughout all this process, you may feel that the board individually and collectively is trying to pierce your defenses, to seek out your hidden weaknesses, and to embarrass and confuse you. Actually, this is not true. They are obliged to make an appraisal of your qualifications for the job you are seeking, and they *want to see you in your best light.* Remember, they must interview all candidates and a noncooperative candidate may become a failure in spite of their best efforts to bring out his qualifications. Here are fifteen(15) suggestions that will help you:

1. <u>Be Natural. Keep Your Attitude Confident,But Not Cocky</u>

If *you* are not confident that you can do the job, do not exexpect the *board* to be. Do not apologize for your weaknesses, try to bring out your strong points. The board is interested in a positive, not a negative presentation. Cockiness will antagonize any board member, and make him wonder if you are covering up a weakness by a false show of strength.

2. <u>Get Comfortable, But Don't Lounge or Sprawl</u>

Sit erectly but not stiffly. A careless posture may lead the board to conclude you are careless in other things, or at least that you are not impressed by the importance of the occasion to you.Either conclusion is natural, even if incorrect. Do not fuss with your clothing, or with a pencil or an ashtray. Your hands may occasionally be useful to emphasize a point; do not let them become a point of distraction.

3. <u>Do Not Wisecrack or Make Small Talk</u>

This is a serious situation, and your attitude should show that you consider it as such. Further, the time of the board is limited; they do not want to waste it, and neither should you.

4. <u>Do Not Exaggerate Your Experience or Abilities</u>

In the first place, from information in the application,from other interviews and other sources, the board may know more about you than you think; in the second place, you probably will not get away with it in the first place. An experienced board is rather adept at spotting such a situation. Do not take the chance.

5. <u>If You Know a Member of the Board, Do Not Make a Point of It, Yet Do Not Hide It.</u>

Certainly you are not fooling him, and probably not the other members of the board. Do not try to take advantage of your acquaintanceship -- it will probably do you little good.

6. <u>Do Not Dominate the Interview</u>

Let the board do that. They will give you the clues -- do not assume that you have to do all the talking. Realize that the board has a number of questions to ask you, and do not try to take up all the interview time by showing off your extensive knowledge of the answer to the first one.

7. Be Attentive

You only have twenty minutes or so, and you should keep your attention at its sharpest throughout. When a member is addressing a problem or a question to you, give him your undivided attention. Address your reply principally to him, but do not exclude the other members of the board.

8. Do Not Interrupt

A board member may be stating a problem for you to analyze. He will ask you a question when the time comes. Let him state the problem, and wait for the question.

9. Make Sure You Understand the Question

Do not try to answer until you are sure what the question is. If it is not clear, restate it in your own words or ask the board member to clarify it for you. But do not haggle about minor elements.

10. Reply Promptly But Not Hastily

A common entry on oral board rating sheets is "candidate responded readily," or "candidate hesitated in replies." Respond as promptly and quickly as you can, but do not jump to a hasty, ill-considered answer.

11. Do Not Be Peremptory in Your Answers

A brief answer is proper -- but do not fire your answer back. That is a losing game from your point of view. The board member can probably ask questions much faster than you can answer them.

12. Do Not Try To Create the Answer You Think the Board Member Wants

He is interested in what kind of · mind you have and how it works -- not in playing games. Furthermore, he can usually spot this practice and will usually grade you down on it.

13. Do Not Switch Sides in Your Reply Merely to Agree With a Board Member

Frequently, a member will take a contrary position merely to draw you out and to see if you are willing and able to defend your point of view. Do not start a debate, yet do not surrender a good position. If a position is worth taking, it is worth defending.

] Do Not Be Afraid to Admit an Error in Judgment if You Are Shown to Be Wrong

The board knows that you are forced to reply without any opportunity for careful consideration. Your answer may be demonstrably wrong. If so, admit it and get on with the interview.

15. Do Not Dwell at Length on Your Present Job

The opening question may relate to your present assignment. Answer the question but do not go into an extended discussion. You are being examined for a *new* job, not your present one. As a matter of fact, try to phrase *all* your answers in terms of the job for which you are being examined.

G. BASIS OF RATING

Probably you will forget most of these "do's" and "don'ts" when you walk into the oral interview room. Even remembering them all will not insure you a passing grade. Perhaps you did not have the qualifications in the first place. But remembering them *will* help you to put your best foot forward, without treading on the toes of the board members.

Rumor and popular opinion to the contrary notwithstanding, an oral board wants you to make the best appearance possible. They know you are under pressure -- but they also want to see how you respond to it as a guide to what your reaction would be under the pressures of the job you seek. They will be influenced by the degree of poise you display, the personal traits you show, and the manner in which you respond.

EXAMINATION SECTION

EXAMINATION SECTION
TEST 1

DIRECTIONS: Each question or incomplete statement is followed by several suggested answers or completions. Select the one that BEST answers the question or completes the statement. *PRINT THE LETTER OF THE CORRECT ANSWER IN THE SPACE AT THE RIGHT.*

1. In working with adolescent groups, an important point to remember is to give   1.___
   A. guidance without taking matters out of the group's hands
   B. guidance to the youth leaders only
   C. assistance only when the groups ask for it
   D. direct assistance at every opportunity

2. The BASIC purpose to be kept in mind when programming group activities for delinquent adolescents is that   2.___
   A. group activities are natural for delinquents
   B. the activities should focus on control and discipline
   C. the youths should share in the program expenses
   D. the activities should focus on total freedom of expression

3. Workers assigned to your unit are experiencing difficulties with programming group activities. The programs seem to be out of context with the problems of the youths, and the youths are reported to be bored, evasive, and non-participating.   3.___
   An important factor in programming that you, as unit supervisor, must teach them is
   A. to involve the group members in the planning and implementation of all programs
   B. to include current procedures like enounter, reality therapy, and crisis intervention
   C. that they must have individual meetings with key members to enlist their aid and assistance
   D. that they are not providing enough direction and control to the group meetings

4. The one of the following groups of characteristics which MOST correctly describes anti-social adolescent groups is   4.___
   A. fraternity, mutual respect, and interest in each other
   B. group loyalty, need to retaliate, and the necessity to fight
   C. divisiveness, mistrust, and self-centeredness
   D. none of the above

5. You are supervising a new worker who tells you, during his supervisory conference, that he feels that he has not been able to help his group to re-direct their energies into productive channels.   5.___

It would be BEST for you to advise this worker that
- A. he should not be discouraged because adolescents have boundless energy that is difficult to control
- B. adolescent groups respond to planning and direction, and that he should set up some simple form of organization
- C. the conflict and competition concept of group behavior requires group psychotherapy
- D. his anxieties are getting in the way of effective work with his group

6. A new worker in the unit under your supervision shows in his recording that he has been able to overcome his feelings of insecurity in his new role of working with his group and to work through the initial testing period imposed on him by the group. However, during his supervisory conference, you discover that he is extremely anxious because the group does not seem to be verbalizing their problems with him.
You should advise this worker in conference that
- A. these are hard-core youths who do not talk about their problems
- B. his recording is weak, and should be done in process style for the next six months
- C. his anxiety is probably being communicated to the group, inhibiting them from verbalizing their problems
- D. a marathon encounter with the group may help them to verbalize their problems

6.___

7. In preparation for a staff conference covering principles of working with alienated youth groups, you assign different aspects of the subject to different workers. In his notes, the worker who is to discuss *process in working with groups* lists the following:
1. sensitivity to the pace of group movement
2. resistance and resentment arising from domination by the worker
3. time and place of meetings
An IMPORTANT part that was omitted by the worker is
- A. realistic programming
- B. awareness of *where the group is at*
- C. the importance of sensitivity training
- D. supervision

7.___

8. A youth worker reports to you in a supervisory conference that the youths in his group are unfriendly and bossy with each other, but that when he leaves them, roughhousing breaks out.
The MOST likely explanation for this is that
- A. he is not exercising enough control
- B. he is probably too strict and tight with them
- C. this particular group of kids usually acts this way
- D. this is unusual behavior of alienated youth

8.___

9. The SIGNIFICANT factors that would distinguish a construc-   9.___
   tive and orderly group of adolescents from an anti-social
   gang are the
      A. aims, quality of the relationships, and behavior of
         the individuals
      B. aims, personality of the members, and locale
      C. age, problems, and behavior of the members
      D. locale, personality of the members, and leadership

10. Youth workers involved with groups of adolescent girls   10.___
    may have to deal with problems of sexual acting-out.
    Programming for girls involved in sexual acting-out
    should have as its BASIC purpose
       A. security building and developing a feeling of being
          needed and wanted
       B. sex information and a discussion of birth control
          and abortion
       C. rap sessions on dating, making out, and male-female
          psychology
       D. parties, dances, outings, and bus rides

11. Adolescents have many fears that they are ashamed to show   11.___
    because they are afraid of disapproval. Restraining these
    fears may lead to anxieties that could be even more
    troublesome.
    To help youths resolve such problems, youth service units
    should emphasize in their programming
       A. activities that help youths gain self-confidence
       B. rap sessions on anxiety
       C. activities that are not likely to produce fear
       D. hiking, swimming, wrestling, and basketball

12. All of the following are purposes of group counseling   12.___
    EXCEPT
       A. avoidance of treating pathology as such
       B. helping clients attain a better level of functioning
       C. modifying social and familial problems
       D. resolving intra-psychic conflicts

13. A MAJOR advantage of having group programs for local   13.___
    teenagers in Youth Services Agency neighborhood offices
    is that
       A. these programs are less expensive to operate
       B. the participating groups are mutual groups in their
          own environment
       C. this activity is necessary for suppressing riots
       D. such programs serve as good public relations

14. A worker reports about his youth council that one of the   14.___
    sub-groups in the council revolves around a boy who has
    many constructive ideas. However, this boy's participa-
    tion is limited due to the rivalry between him and the
    elected president.

The supervisor should advise the worker to
  A. have the leader of the sub-group excluded from the council
  B. help the leader of the sub-group participate more actively
  C. tell the leader of the sub-group to *play ball* with the rest of the council
  D. let the council settle this problem without outside assistance

15. One of your youth workers is having difficulty forming a group in a particular neighborhood. Parents in that area are upset about the idea of teenage groups. This worker plans to meet with some of these parents, and he asks your help in reaching a goal with them.
As supervisor, you should advise him to approach this problem by
  A. helping the parents to see that group activities are a sign of a youth's growth, not of a lack of gratitude or affection for his parents
  B. informing the parents that it is the professional opinion of the Youth Services Agency that groups are necessary in order to serve youth constructively
  C. postponing this meeting until you can convince individual parents of the value of groups
  D. helping the parents to see that many of their teenagers are having difficulties at home and in school because they do not participate in group activities

15.___

16. Experts have described festivals, fairs, holidays, etc. as *nothing less nor more than excesses provided by law and which owe their cheerful character to the release which they bring.*
The significance of this in programming unit projects is to
  A. have the workers assist the community in sponsoring fairs, block dances, etc.
  B. leave the sponsoring of fairs, dances, etc. to associations affiliated with the police department
  C. avoid involving large groups of people in public affairs because of the danger of fights, riots, etc.
  D. use a good part of the unit's budget for fairs, dances, bazaars, etc.

16.___

17. Which one of the groups listed below has the following four characteristics:
  1. Basic depressive character
  2. Intolerance for frustration and pain
  3. Lack of meaningful objects
  4. Artificial technique to maintain self-regard?

  A. College students   B. Drug abusers
  C. Adolescents   D. Alienated youth

17.___

18. The MOST important consideration in evaluating the ego   18.___
    strength of an angry, deprived, mistreated, frustrated,
    evasive client is the client's ability to
       A. verbalize his problems
       B. redirect his anger
       C. form a relationship with an accepting worker
       D. hold a job

19. When a worker, in his first interview with a parent, tries   19.___
    to take down a developmental history of a boy, he usually
    gets many meaningless answers, such as *It was normal* or
    I don't remember.
    The worker should realize that
       A. this information is inaccurate and should be dis-
          regarded
       B. the parent is under stress at first, and should be
          able to give more factual information later
       C. the parent purposely is withholding valuable infor-
          mation about the boy
       D. the parent must be told that if he cannot cooperate
          he cannot be helped

20. One of the workers under your supervision is puzzled as   20.___
    to why a mother she was working with broke off contacts
    prematurely. When you read the record of this mother,
    you learn that she had become overdependent upon the
    worker before suddenly stopping her visits.
    In the supervisory conference, you should help the
    worker to understand that this type of client
       A. is flighty, evasive, and has low reality testing
       B. is in need of deep psychotherapy
       C. is defending herself against this overdependence
       D. needs the chance to test her limits with an accept-
          ing person

21. When a worker is troubled because youths in his group   21.___
    ask him personal questions and he does not know how to
    answer them, as unit supervisor it would be BEST for
    you to advise the worker to
       A. interrogate the youths in detail about the reasons
          behind the questions
       B. tell the youths all they want to know, so that the
          worker appears friendly and human
       C. give a frank, brief, truthful answer and then imme-
          diately redirect the youths back to their own
          problems
       D. point out to the youths that the worker's personal
          life is not their business

22. Psychiatrists are usually concerned with the total func-   22.___
    tioning and integration of the human personality.
    Caseworkers usually concentrate on
       A. the same thing, but for shorter periods of time
       B. the same thing, but without prescribing medication
       C. helping the client to deal with the presenting
          problem
       D. all of the above

23. Some people feel that by cutting down temptations and
stimuli, delinquency can be substantially decreased.
Specific measures are curfews, eliminating the cruder
forms of violence from the mass media, reducing the
number of sexually stimulating publications available
to youth, keeping down teenagers' resources for obtaining
liquor, increasing recreational facilities, etc.
The STRONGEST flaw in this approach is that
    A. it is not fair to non-delinquents
    B. it would not seriously affect the hard-core delin-
       quent
    C. the community is not yet prepared for it
    D. it needs more time to prove itself

23.___

24. A COMMON error made by youth workers who are beginning
to find out about the influence of unconscious desires
and emotions on human behavior is to
    A. probe the client unnecessarily
    B. become over-assured that they can solve the client's
       problem
    C. slow up the pace of the interview
    D. look for the proper treatment method based on the
       client's neurosis

24.___

25. A basic technique which is used to obtain knowledge of
the problem to be solved and sufficient understanding of
the troubled person and of the situation, so that the
problem can be solved effectively, is known as
    A. psychosomatics   B. interviewing
    C. recording   D. supervisory conferences

25.___

26. Which of the following is a CORRECT definition of the
term *acceptance* as used in social work?
    A. A decision made at intake to accept the client as a
       case for the agency to handle
    B. The concept that the worker does not pass judgment
       on the client's behavior
    C. The concept of a positive and active understanding
       by the worker of the feelings a client expresses
       through his behavior
    D. Communication to the client that the worker does
       not condone and accept his anti-social behavior

26.___

27. Beginning youth workers are usually informed in a training
session that they should be non-judgmental, should not
become dependent on the client's liking them, and should
not become angry. However, in an attempt to suppress
these feelings, workers often behave in a stilted and
artificial manner with clients.
As a supervisor, you should help your workers
    A. seek counseling to help them understand their angry
       feelings
    B. realize that they were not yet ready for that type
       of training

27.___

C. understand that this artificiality will soon pass by
   as easily as it came
D. recognize the naturalness of these feelings and learn
   to control their expression

28. A worker in the unit under your supervision has a youth   28.___
in his group who has developed a strong antagonism toward
him. You can find nothing that the worker has done to
arouse such antagonism in the youth.
This antagonism is probably due to
   A. restrictions imposed on the client by the agency
   B. factors deeply hidden in the client's personality
   C. the youth's feeling of guilt because he has with-
      held information from the worker
   D. the fact that the worker may have promised the
      youth too much

29. The development of an emotional rapport, positive or   29.___
negative, between the client and the worker is not abnor-
mal, but inevitable. Sometimes the feelings that develop
as a result of this rapport become excessively intense.
In those instances, the worker should
   A. request that the client be given another worker
   B. control the nature and intensity of the feelings
   C. ignore the feelings, which will disappear soon
   D. confront the client with the inappropriateness of
      these feelings

30. In social work, when we talk of ambivalence, we mean that   30.___
the
   A. social worker refrains from imposing his moral judg-
      ments on the client
   B. supervisor assists the worker in understanding the
      psychological causes for client's behavior
   C. client has conflicting interests, desires, and
      emotions
   D. client is seeking someone who will understand the
      subjective reasons for his behavior

31. Although we can judge statements about objectively veri-   31.___
fiable matters to be true or false, we are not similarly
justified in passing judgments on subjective attitudes.
This statement BEST explains the rationale behind the
social work principle of
   A. empathy   B. self-awareness
   C. non-judgmentality   D. confidentiality

32. A psychological factor that explains why generally law-   32.___
abiding individuals can become a part of a violent crowd
is
   A. the deep urge for destruction and violence inherent
      in man
   B. the anonymity of the group would allow individuals
      to yield to restrained instincts

    C. that there is force in numbers, decreasing the like-
       lihood of personal injury
    D. that man is basically a *herd animal*, so the mob is
       our natural environment

33. When you have learned that one of your workers has
    organized a protest, you should advise him to
    A. be aware that the group may not be able to defend
       themselves against the police
    B. alert the community to distract the police to
       another area
    C. call off the protest because of the probability of
       danger
    D. take precautions with his group in order to be sure
       that the protest will be orderly
                                           33.___

34. Some local merchants are disturbed because they feel that
    a group of boys who *hang on the corner* will develop into
    a delinquent gang. They invite you, the unit supervisor,
    to address them at a meeting in order to describe the
    characteristics of delinquent gangs to them.
    In your talk to these merchants, you should
    A. describe how delinquent gangs make a career of hang-
       ing around, have a blind loyalty among members, and
       see destruction as their way of hitting back at
       society
    B. advise them to call off the meeting because the
       delinquent gang as such has disappeared
    C. assure them that they should not be concerned
       because you have a worker in that area who has this
       group under surveillance
    D. contact your area administrator because this
       involves a relationship with the community that is
       not on your level of responsibility
                                           34.___

35. According to the REPORT OF THE NATIONAL ADVISORY COMMIT-
    TEE ON CIVIL DISORDERS, riots are dramatic forms of
    protest expressing
    A. hostility to government or private institutions
    B. undefined but real frustrations
    C. anger at the failure of society to provide certain
       groups with adequate opportunities
    D. all of the above
                                           35.___

36. Many neighborhoods seem to develop a subculture in which
    forms of criminal and delinquent behavior and values are
    accepted as norms.
    If the unit area happens to be in one of these neighbor-
    hoods, the unit supervisor would be BEST advised to keep
    in mind that
    A. we know less about changing subcultures than we know
       about influencing groups and individuals
    B. it is easier to change subcultures than to influence
       groups and individuals
                                         36.___

C. subcultures are simple to identify, and helping the members to resolve their problems is comparatively easy

D. this is only a theory and, therefore, should not influence the functioning of the unit office

37. The neighborhood drug abuse prevention network of the
Addiction Services Agency is a series of broad-based
community groups called
   A. CARE AND AWARE   B. EVIL AND WEAK
   C. RARE AND AWARE   D. NACE AND CARE

37.___

38. An agency whose sole purpose is to fight addiction
through a comprehensive prevention and rehabilitation
program is
   A. Daytop Village
   B. Narcotics Addiction Control Commission
   C. Addiction Services Agency
   D. Phoenix House

38.___

39. Agencies which have been traditionally used by the Youth
Services Agency for the purpose of sponsoring approved
group programs to help youth improve their behavior are:
   A. Madison-Felicia, Vocational Advisory Service, Catholic
      Youth Organization, United Neighborhood Houses,
      Federation Employment and Guidance Service, Community
      Centers
   B. Office of Economic Opportunity, Catholic Youth
      Organization, Police Athletic League, Federation
      Employment and Guidance Service, Vocational Advisory
      Service, Jewish Family Service, Federation of
      Protestant Welfare Agencies
   C. Catholic Youth Organization, United Neighborhood
      Houses, Young Men's Christian Association, Protes-
      tant Council, Police Athletic League, Builders For
      the Family and Youth
   D. Catholic Youth Organization, Young Men's Christian
      Association, Protestant Council, Police Athletic
      League, Office of Economic Opportunity, Builders For
      Family and Youth, Vocational Advisory Service

39.___

40. Agencies that are used by Youth Services Agency to provide
individual casework treatment services for Youth Services
Agency clients who need individual therapy for deep-
seated problems are:
   A. Jewish Family Services, State Division for Youth,
      Catholic Charities, Staten Island Family Service,
      Salvation Army, Community Education
   B. Big Brothers, Catholic Charities, Jewish Board of
      Guardians, Jewish Family Services, Salvation Army
   C. Catholic Youth Organization, Vocational Advisory
      Service, Melrose Center, Federation Employment and
      Guidance Service, United Neighborhood Houses
   D. Catholic Charities, Jewish Family Service, Vocational
      Foundation, Vermont Program, Big Brothers, Boys'
      Harbor, Salvation Army

40.___

41. The Departments that make up the Human Resources Adminis-   41.___
    tration are:
    A. Manpower and Career Development, Office of Economic
       Opportunity, Commission on Civil Disorders, Youth
       Services Agency, Addiction Services, Social Services,
       Community Development
    B. Manpower and Career Development Agency, Office of
       Economic Opportunity, Youth Services Agency, Addic-
       tion Services Agency, Department of Social Services,
       Commission on Human Rights, Community Volunteers
    C. Human Resources Administration Central Staff, Man-
       power and Career Development Agency, Community
       Development Agency, Department of Social Services,
       Youth Services Agency, Addiction Services Agency,
       Office of Education Affairs
    D. Human Resources Administration Central Staff, Man-
       power and Career Development Agency, Department of
       Social Services, Youth Services Agency, Addiction
       Services Agency, Office of Economic Opportunity,
       Commission on Human Rights

42. A Youth Services Agency project that was developed in   42.___
    1968 in response to the findings of the National Advisory
    Commission on Civil Disorders (Kerner-Lindsay Report)
    and which was designed to develop and demonstrate model
    approaches to engender interracial understanding between
    teenagers is the
    A. Youth Opportunity Center
    B. Demonstration and Training Unit
    C. Interdepartmental Neighborhood Service Center
    D. Vermont Project

43. Which one of the following is mandated to provide ser-   43.___
    vices to the poverty-stricken, to improve the quality of
    these services and the methods of delivering them, to
    carry out the legal commitment to the poor, and to help
    the poor to help themselves?
    A. Office of Economic Opportunity
    B. Environmental Resources Administration
    C. Community Action Program
    D. Model Cities Program

44. An indication of mature behavior to be sought for in the   44.___
    client and encouraged by the youth worker is the
    A. ability to become involved in issues of racism,
       urban life, and human rights
    B. development of some controls over the impulse to
       act out
    C. formulation of definite and specific goals in
       careers
    D. steady, consistent pattern of behavior that is
       relatively free of ambivalent feelings

45. That point in human development which marks a person's 45.___
passage into adolescence is known as
   A. maturity   B. the Oedipal stage
   C. the genital stage   D. puberty

46. An important factor to remember about the mental, physi- 46.___
cal, social, and emotional growth of an adolescent is
that the
   A. pace is uneven and individual
   B. pace is relatively even
   C. rate of growth is predictable
   D. growth has no special pattern

47. Adolescents are more likely to understand the concrete 47.___
and the specific, rather than general ideas like justice,
honesty, love, etc.
The implication of this concept for the unit supervisor
in guiding his staff is
   A. that programming should include recreation, job
      counseling, school help, and visits at times of
      crisis
   B. the necessity to make sure that the programs use a
      large part of their budget for *treats* for the youth
   C. to be sure the staff is directing much of their
      energy into pointing up the importance of these
      general concepts
   D. to help the youths understand that life has taught
      them to be mistrustful

48. The theory of juvenile delinquency that traces much of 48.___
delinquency back to failures in family relationships
during the early years of childhood, and to continuing
family difficulties, offers help to the youth worker in
   A. forming a general picture of the typical delinquent
   B. understanding that fighting is one of the best ways
      to rise to the top
   C. identifying normal growth needs of adolescents and
      the obstacles against healthy maturity
   D. realizing that delinquents are children at heart and
      are best treated as children

49. The theory of juvenile delinquency which holds that 49.___
youths from minority groups turn to anti-social behavior
when they feel that their access to social, educational,
and economic opportunities in legal and approved ways is
blocked has had a strong impact on the establishment of
agencies like the
   A. Job Corps
   B. Community Development Agency
   C. Youth Board of the 1950's
   D. Addiction Services Agency

50. Which of the following is a descriptive term for a client   50.___
    who is resistive, breaks appointments, withholds informa-
    tion, beclouds issues, relates to others in a primitive,
    often distorted, fashion, and acts out his wishes and
    conflicts in his contact with the worker?
    A. Psychotic   B. Narcotics addict
    C. Schizophrenic   D. Character disorder

————

KEY (CORRECT ANSWERS)

1. A	11. A	21. C	31. C	41. C
2. B	12. D	22. C	32. B	42. D
3. A	13. B	23. B	33. D	43. A
4. B	14. B	24. A	34. A	44. B
5. B	15. A	25. B	35. D	45. D
6. C	16. A	26. C	36. A	46. A
7. A	17. B	27. D	37. C	47. A
8. B	18. C	28. B	38. C	48. C
9. A	19. B	29. B	39. C	49. A
10. A	20. C	30. C	40. B	50. D

————

TEST 2

DIRECTIONS: Each question or incomplete statement is followed by several suggested answers or completions. Select the one that BEST answers the question or completes the statement. *PRINT THE LETTER OF THE CORRECT ANSWER IN THE SPACE AT THE RIGHT.*

1. Adolescents who become involved in delinquent behavior are usually angry or frustrated a large part of their time. Conscious awareness of the intensity of their needs makes them feel weak.
   For this reason, they frequently
   A. are easier to work with
   B. prefer strong male youth workers
   C. need to be controlled and disciplined
   D. have to show the world they don't care what happens

   1.___

2. Sociologists and behavioral scientists provided the ideas of cohesion, conflict, competition, cooperation, authority, leadership, and stratification that are clearly manifested in
   A. supervision   B. addiction
   C. group behavior   D. casework therapy

   2.___

3. The one of the following causes of juvenile delinquency among sub-lower class youth which has been given increased attention in recent years is the
   A. prevalence of the one-parent family
   B. failure of family relationships in the early years
   C. blockage of educational, vocational, and social opportunities
   D. emotional problems and psychiatric disorders of youth

   3.___

4. A high-ranking official recently stated that some youths have made suicide attempts in detention centers so that they would be transferred from the detention centers to hospitals.
   If the workers in a unit should bring this topic up for discussion in a staff meeting, the supervisor should
   A. instruct workers to inform the youths of the area about this method of getting out of a detention center
   B. have a worker visit a youth in detention in order to observe and report back to the unit so that a demonstration can be organized
   C. assign different workers to study various aspects of the problem in order to plan an intelligent, informed discussion
   D. point out that the worker does not directly become involved with this problem, and direct the discussion to a more pertinent topic

   4.___

5. The MOST significant characteristics of the daily lives   5.___
   of alienated youths can be described as
     A. their days are aimless, disorganized, and unproduc-
        tive
     B. they spend most of their time in anti-social activity
     C. they spend a good portion of their time seeking a
        means of earning money
     D. they concentrate most of their energies on acting-
        out

6. A young man drops into the office to request help in   6.___
   finding a job. While he is waiting to see the office
   coverage worker, you notice he is nervous, sweating,
   yawning, and constantly blowing his nose.
   As a unit supervisor, you should
     A. overlook this because the youth is probably worried
        about getting a job, and is dirty and tired
     B. feel assured that the worker will observe this also
        and handle it in the best possible way
     C. advise the worker of your observations, and discuss
        the possible causes of this behavior with the worker
     D. do none of the above

7. The *battered child syndrome* is reported to be one of the   7.___
   most difficult problems facing health officials.
   When a worker knows of a case of a boy being severely
   abused physically by his parents, the supervisor should
   advise the worker to
     A. discuss this with a psychiatrist to find out why the
        parent is abusing the child
     B. tell the child to stay away from the parents as much
        as possible
     C. try to talk to the parents to help them see what
        they are doing wrong
     D. report the situation to the Bureau of Child Welfare
        of the Department of Social Services

8. Ghetto youth today present symptoms of delinquent   8.___
   behavior that are in many ways more disruptive than
   those of the anti-social gang members of the 1950's.
   Some of these symptoms are
     A. alienation, school drop-outs, drug addiction,
        loosely formed cliques
     B. interracial conflicts, community violence, few
        family ties, teenage drifters, and panhandlers
     C. promiscuity, alcoholism, vandalism, homosexuality,
        venereal disease
     D. all of the above

9. A psychological factor that tends to make the spread of   9.___
   drug abuse today easier among siblings in a family is the
     A. necessity for drug users to seduce others to join them
     B. need of siblings to rebel against parents
     C. fact that siblings can more easily *cover* for each
        other
     D. fact that older siblings can force younger siblings
        to take drugs

10. A parent complains to a worker that her teenage son is   10.___
    hanging around with a *bad bunch*, that money is strangely
    missing from the house lately, that his eating habits
    have changed, and that he spends long periods of time
    alone.
    When the worker discusses this with the unit supervisor,
    the supervisor should
       A. interview the parent as soon as possible to get more
          precise information
       B. advise the worker to refer the parent to a doctor
          to have her son examined
      \ C. help the worker to be supportive to the parent and
          try to make contact with the son
       D. assure him the parent is just jumpy over the drug
          scare and there is probably another explanation for
          the boy's behavior

11. A worker reports that the youths in his area think that   11.___
    blowing pot is all right because marijuana is not addic-
    tive, is harmless in small doses, and is far less dan-
    gerous than alcohol. The worker asks your help to talk
    the kids out of *blowing pot*.
    You, as unit supervisor, should
       A. advise the worker to refer the youths to the nearest,
          best drug rehabilitation resource
       B. give the worker enough literature so the youths
          could learn more about the situation
       C. assure the worker that these facts are true
      \ D. help the worker to involve the youths in construc-
          tive group activities

12. It is important for the youth worker to understand that   12.___
    the adolescent's FIRST loyalty belongs to his
      \ A. peer group   B. siblings
       C. parents   D. best friend

13. One of the workers in a unit office reports that he is   13.___
    having some difficulty with his group of youths. It is
    apparent that the youth leader of the group is seriously
    disturbed.
    The BEST action for the worker to take FIRST is to
       A. try to redirect the leader's activities into more
          constructive channels
       B. help the group select a leader who is more psycho-
          logically sound
      \ C. take steps to have the leader removed from the
          community into a setting where he can get psychia-
          tric help
       D. show this leader where his behavior is hurting the
          group so that he can change his behavior

14. The pleasurable effect produced by heroin is the   14.___
       A. feeling of excitement and energy
       B. expansion of sense perceptions
       C. feeling of relaxation, sociability, and good humor
      \ D. suppression of fears, tensions, and anxieties

15. The many rumors that spread throughout the Youth Services   15.___
    Agency are harmful to the morale of the staff because they
    result in worry, suspicion, mistrust, and uncertainty.
    The BEST way the unit supervisor can stop a rumor is to
        A. disregard it
        B. deny it
        C. start a different one
        D. give the staff the true facts

16. Parental rejection and neglect damage the personality of   16.___
    the developing child, and orient the child toward his
    agemates in the neighborhood.
    This statement would BEST describe the mechanism that
    leads to
        A. delinquency in urban industrial areas
        B. the establishment of neighborhood clubs
        C. the generation gap
        D. drug addiction

17. Many young people are introduced to drugs by friends.   17.___
    Youths don't like to be called *chicken*, they like to be
    hip like the rest, and they have to be a part of some-
    thing.
    When a worker asks for your guidance on handling one of
    his youths who is being pressured into getting *high* by
    his friends, as the unit supervisor, you should help the
    worker
        A. gradually move this youth into another group of
           youths who are *straight*
        B. make the worker realize this is his problem, in
           his area, and that he must work it out the best way
        C. involve this youth and his group of friends in the
           programs and activities of the unit
        D. tell the youth he must work this out himself

18. Youth workers must help angry alienated adolescents to   18.___
    learn how to
        A. control their anger by learning when it's worthwhile
           to get angry
        B. suppress their angry feelings
        C. realize that anger is an unconscious emotion
        D. take part in aggressive demonstrations and takeovers

19. Of the following, an IMPORTANT reason why certain youths   19.___
    are stereotyped by the police and are therefore treated
    unfairly by them is that
        A. delinquent youths deserve to be treated more severely
           because they cause trouble for others
        B. these are only allegations and rhetoric made up by
           revolutionary elements who are hostile to the police
        C. the prevalence of *turnstile justice* results in hasty
           judgments by the police
        D. police officers in the field have no immediate data
           concerning the youths' backgrounds and react to
           their behavior at the moment

20. Group approaches are COMMONLY used for   20.___
    A. encounter, discussion, training, and administration
    B. education, counseling, therapy, and recreation
    C. counseling, recreation, catharsis, and crisis inter-
       vention
    D. competition, leadership, administration, and training

21. A worker under your supervision is having difficulty   21.___
reaching some of the youths he is working with on a one-
to-one basis. The recording on these youths shows that
they have had little opportunity for healthy interpersonal
relations.
You should advise this worker to
    A. involve these youths in group counseling in order to
       help them overcome their reluctance in sharing
       experiences with another person
    B. refer these youths for psychiatric services because
       they are not likely to be reached by a youth worker
    C. assign these youths to Big Brothers or Big Sisters
       because they need to share a normal family experi-
       ence
    D. give these youths more time to get to know and trust
       the worker

22. Planning, organization, methods, direction, coordination,   22.___
budget and fiscal management, public relations, personnel
administration, training, and supervision are the
ESSENTIAL elements of
    A. group psychotherapy   B. ego-oriented casework
    C. consultation   D. administration

23. If a supervisor is unaware of a new worker's limitations   23.___
and makes demands which are beyond the worker's capabilities, this will
    A. undermine the worker's confidence in functioning up
       to the limit of his actual capacities
    B. provide an incentive for the worker to further his
       training and improve services
    C. demonstrate the need for the agency to provide
       better orientation and in-service training for staff
    D. encourage the worker to function at a level higher
       than his present capacities

24. A high government official has announced: *We're looking*   24.___
for possible consolidation of services, for overlapping,
for frills, for some built-in bureacratic procedures that
have been kind of historic but that no one has ever taken
a long look at to see if time and technology have made
them obsolete.
For the unit supervisor, the implication of this statement is that it is his responsibility to
    A. ignore this announcement since it pertains to matters
       beyond his responsibility
    B. report all matters of bureaucratic inefficiency
       directly to this high government official

C. inform his workers at a staff meeting that there will
be no funds for programs for the next few months
D. try to involve the staff in a realistic reappraisal
of the unit's program and discuss suggestions for
cutbacks with the area administrator

25. Assume that you are a new unit supervisor in the Youth   25.___
Services Agency and your workers bring many grievances
to your attention.
The BEST way for you, the supervisor, to reduce grievances
in your unit is to
A. have the workers submit fully documented written
grievances
B. consider each grievance seriously and eliminate the
cause if possible
C. make workers realize that grievances reflect their
immaturity and rejection of authority
D. refer the workers' grievances to the Area Administrator

26. Of the following, BASIC subject areas to be discussed in   26.___
staff conferences are:
A. Job responsibilities, agency structure, social work
concepts, needs and resources of people
B. Case-studying, interviewing, individual growth and
development, sources of information other than the
client
C. Community resources, work organization, child
welfare services, and standards of performance
D. All of the above

27. The discussion method in teaching provides a way to help   27.___
staff integrate knowledge and thus make it available for
application to day-to-day work.
To help workers integrate knowledge and develop skill
is an IMPORTANT aspect of
A. professional training
B. memos, directives, and position papers
C. staff and individual conferences
D. job descriptions

28. The subjects of discussion in staff meetings cannot be   28.___
isolated from what the unit supervisor
A. thinks is most important
B. reads in books, journals, etc.
C. hears at supervisors' meetings
D. discusses in individual conferences

29. Interplay between persons appears to speed up the learn-   29.___
ing process; discussion of the material provides an
opportunity for a sharing of knowledge and experience
and allows for a testing out of new ideas and application
of theory.

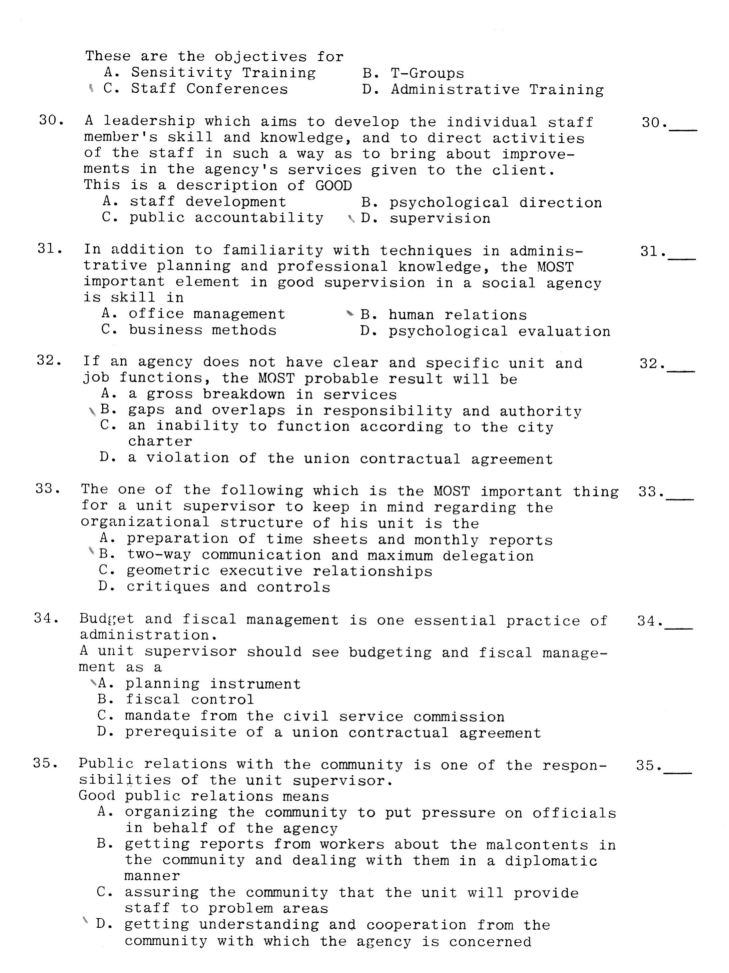

These are the objectives for
   A. Sensitivity Training   B. T-Groups
   C. Staff Conferences   D. Administrative Training

30. A leadership which aims to develop the individual staff   30.___
member's skill and knowledge, and to direct activities
of the staff in such a way as to bring about improvements in the agency's services given to the client.
This is a description of GOOD
   A. staff development   B. psychological direction
   C. public accountability   D. supervision

31. In addition to familiarity with techniques in adminis-   31.___
trative planning and professional knowledge, the MOST
important element in good supervision in a social agency
is skill in
   A. office management   B. human relations
   C. business methods   D. psychological evaluation

32. If an agency does not have clear and specific unit and   32.___
job functions, the MOST probable result will be
   A. a gross breakdown in services
   B. gaps and overlaps in responsibility and authority
   C. an inability to function according to the city
      charter
   D. a violation of the union contractual agreement

33. The one of the following which is the MOST important thing   33.___
for a unit supervisor to keep in mind regarding the
organizational structure of his unit is the
   A. preparation of time sheets and monthly reports
   B. two-way communication and maximum delegation
   C. geometric executive relationships
   D. critiques and controls

34. Budget and fiscal management is one essential practice of   34.___
administration.
A unit supervisor should see budgeting and fiscal manage-
ment as a
   A. planning instrument
   B. fiscal control
   C. mandate from the civil service commission
   D. prerequisite of a union contractual agreement

35. Public relations with the community is one of the respon-   35.___
sibilities of the unit supervisor.
Good public relations means
   A. organizing the community to put pressure on officials
      in behalf of the agency
   B. getting reports from workers about the malcontents in
      the community and dealing with them in a diplomatic
      manner
   C. assuring the community that the unit will provide
      staff to problem areas
   D. getting understanding and cooperation from the
      community with which the agency is concerned

36. Problems and misunderstandings that arise from the lack   36.___
of effective intraorganizational communication are
apparent in many organizations.
Of the following, the means to be employed by the unit
supervisor to establish effective communication are
    A. supervisory and staff conferences
    B. manuals, bulletins, and periodic reports
    C. bulletin boards, memos, and unit newsletters
    \D. all of the above

37. A personnel problem facing supervisors in public service   37.___
more than in private industry is
    A. union management and negotiation
    B. budget and fiscal control
    \C. systematic selection and tenure
    D. advisory boards and political connections

38. Which of the following three types of records are COMMON   38.___
to most social agencies?
    A. Administrative, budgetary, and case
    \B. Administrative, statistical, and case
    C. Administrative, budgetary, and statistical
    D. Budgetary, statistical, and case

39. Even after several supervisory conferences on a case, a   39.___
worker in your unit seems not to be giving effective help.
In a burst of anger, the worker tells a coworker that the
supervisor expects him to learn in a short time what the
supervisor has taken years to learn.
Of the following, the BEST description of the supervisory
relationship here is that the
    \A. supervisor is so intent on seeing that the necessary
       service is given that he is unaware of the worker's
       inability to perform the service
    B. worker's behavior shows that he is too immature to
       be working in such a difficult field
    C. worker is unaware of casework principles and tech-
       niques and their application to such a difficult case
    D. supervisor is unable to give the worker effective
       guidance in the supervisory conference, which
       indicates that the worker needs academic professional
       training

40. The one of the following which is NOT an essential ingre-   40.___
dient of a good staff development and training program
is that it should
    A. include all members of the agency
    B. meet the specific needs of the staff in relation to
       their job responsibilities
    C. be a continuing process
    D. give out the necessary rules and regulations of the
       agency

41. One of the areas in which consultation differs from   41.___
    supervision is that consultation
       A. is not in the direct administrative line of authority
       B. is offered by someone skilled in a specific area
       C. relates to procedure rather than function
       D. requires special training

42. The supervisor should make sure the unit office keeps   42.___
    records about the youths it serves and their families
    since these records help in diagnosing and understanding
    the problems.
    Of the following, as the PRIMARY source of information
    for case records, the workers should use
       A. reports from psychiatrists, doctors, etc.
       B. all other agencies involved with the family
       C. teachers, friends, local indigenous leaders
       D. the parents and the youths themselves

43. Statistical records are needed for planning, research,   43.___
    and accountability although many workers feel that statis-
    tics are dull and boring.
    On the unit level, statistics can come alive when they are
       A. recorded in non-technical language
       B. compiled by the unit expert in mathematics
       C. collected selectively and used against a background
          knowledge of the community
       D. elaborate, detailed, and accurate

44. With the passage of time, case records   44.___
       A. become more valuable
       B. decline in usefulness
       C. produce more information
       D. become cumulative records

45. In general, the purpose of a case record is to   45.___
       A. improve staff training and development
       B. make statistics pertinent and real
       C. provide data for research
       D. further professional service to a client

46. A unit supervisor finds after an intensive in-service   46.___
    training course in case recording that his workers tend
    to postpone their recording and summaries.
    The MOST likely explanation for this is that
       A. recording is not valuable enough to waste that amount
          of time on
       B. sufficient leadership was not given in the develop-
          ment of case records
       C. the workers are too busy in the field to have time
          to record
       D. the latest trend in social work is towards shorter
          records

47. A unit supervisor who has fewer youth workers in his unit than he can supervise effectively will be likely to
    A. make his staff overdependent on him
    B. lack the desire to train his workers effectively
    C. confuse his staff because of lack of direction
    D. supervise his staff too closely

48. The one of the following which is MOST likely to be seriously impaired as a result of poor supervision is the
    A. attitude of youth workers
    B. area of inter-departmental relations
    C. maintenance of case records and reports
    D. staff training and development program

49. It is generally good practice for the supervisor to ask for the opinions of his staff members before taking action affecting them.
    The GREATEST disadvantage of following this principle when changing schedules or assignments is that staff may
    A. believe that the supervisor is unable to make his own decisions
    B. take advantage of the opportunity to present grievances during the discussion
    C. be resentful if their suggestions are not accepted
    D. suggest the same action as the supervisor had planned to take

50. The expansion of community relations or human relations units is a development resulting from the ghetto riots of the past few years.
    The MOST important function such a unit can perform is to
    A. preach brotherhood and racial equality
    B. serve as a means for local city agency officials to develop city policy in accordance with local needs
    C. serve as a means of communication between people with grievances and policy makers who can take action
    D. give awards to prominent citizens who have promoted inter-racial understanding

KEY (CORRECT ANSWERS)

1. D	11. D	21. A	31. B	41. A
2. C	12. A	22. D	32. B	42. D
3. C	13. C	23. A	33. B	43. C
4. C	14. D	24. D	34. A	44. B
5. A	15. D	25. B	35. D	45. D
6. C	16. A	26. D	36. D	46. B
7. D	17. C	27. C	37. C	47. D
8. D	18. A	28. D	38. B	48. A
9. A	19. D	29. C	39. A	49. C
10. C	20. B	30. D	40. A	50. C

EXAMINATION SECTION
TEST 1

DIRECTIONS: Each question or incomplete statement is followed by several suggested answers or completions. Select the one that BEST answers the question or completes the statement. *PRINT THE LETTER OF THE CORRECT ANSWER IN THE SPACE AT THE RIGHT.*

1. The statement that the youth worker may be used by the members of his gang group as a *role model* means MOST NEARLY that the members may
   A. adopt the worker's behavior, attitudes, and beliefs as their own standards
   B. conceal their roles in the gang from the worker in order to gain his acceptance and trust
   C. test the worker by *acting out* on purpose
   D. conceal their roles in the gang from the worker in order to confuse him

1.___

2. Which of the following statements about the categories of gang members is CORRECT?
   A
   A. peripheral member does not participate in gang con- flict with core members
   B. core member is defined as a leader of the gang
   C. peripheral member is an informal gang leader
   D. core member is a full-fledged, accepted member of the gang

2.___

3. An uncooperative and antagonistic attitude among adult groups toward youth workers seeking to modify criminal patterns of behavior among youth gang groups is MOST likely to be prevalent in a neighborhood where
   A. efforts of youth-serving agencies long established in the community have produced no tangible results
   B. significant segments of the adult population engage in or support various types of criminal activity
   C. powerful middle-class elements of the population refuse to openly admit the existence of anti-social youth groups, for fear of giving the neighborhood a bad reputation
   D. behavior patterns of gang groups are extremely aggressive and destructive of life and property in the neighborhood

3.___

4. The characteristics of the groups to be served are a major consideration in developing programs for delinquent youth.
   In general, it has been found that the anti-social acts of juvenile delinquents in neighborhoods that are lowest on the socio-economic scale, compared to the anti-social acts of juvenile delinquents in less deprived areas, are
   A. more aggressive   B. less aggressive
   C. more organized   D. easier to control

4.___

5. The peer group is even more important for the delinquent   5.___
    adolescent who comes from a severely disadvantaged back-
    ground than for the comparatively normal middle-class
    adolescent, MAINLY because the peer group provides the
    delinquent adolescent with
    A. protection from a usually extreme sense of failure
       resulting from defective family, school, and other
       relationships
    B. ways of obtaining needed funds by participating with
       their peers in such anti-social acts as muggings,
       robbery, and petty larceny
    C. opportunities to participate in recreational activi-
       ties that are usually available only to middle-class
       adolescents
    D. access to preparation for realistic adult goals in
       such legitimate occupations as construction worker,
       dock worker, or other unskilled and semi-skilled jobs

6. A street-based youth services program is more exposed to   6.___
    community view and evaluation than a program based in a
    community center or other indoor meeting place. There-
    fore, there is greater risk of community disapproval and
    loss of support.
    Of the following, the BEST way to minimize this risk is
    for the agency sponsoring a street-based program to
    A. make every effort to withhold information from the
       community about such incidents as gang fights,
       homicides, and criminal activities involving youth
    B. interpret the nature of the service to the community
       clearly and objectively, giving information about
       both negative and positive results of the program
    C. arrange for neighborhood gang groups to congregate
       in their clubrooms wherever possible, so that their
       activities will not be exposed to view
    D. insist that the police enforce strong punitive
       measures when gang groups commit anti-social acts
       that may cause community disapproval of a street-
       based program

7. Which of the following statements about differences in   7.___
    attitudes and reactions toward delinquent behavior is
    NOT valid?
    Behavior
    A. viewed as delinquent in a middle-class neighborhood
       may not be so regarded in a lower-class neighborhood
    B. considered delinquent in one lower-class neighbor-
       hood may be regarded with less concern in another
       lower-class neighborhood
    C. which a youth worker considers delinquent and attempts
       to change when he has established a positive rela-
       tionship with a gang group would be handled different-
       ly during his early contacts with the group
    D. which a youth worker considers delinquent and attempts
       to change during his early contacts with a gang group
       would be treated more leniently when he has established
       a positive relationship with the group

8. The area approach to street work is oriented more toward   8.___
   sociological theory than social work. It rests on the
   assumption that delinquent gangs reflect the normal striv-
   ings of groups of youngsters whose opportunities for
   acceptable behavior are limited.
   The one of the following which is MOST likely to be the
   major emphasis of practitioners of the area approach to
   street work with youth is to
       A. preserve the gang structure and provide intensive
          supportive counseling services to individual members
          and their families
       B. undermine the gang structure and provide intensive
          supportive counseling services to members and their
          families
       C. preserve the gang structure and provide more oppor-
          tunities for gang members to channel their behavior
          into constructive activities
       D. undermine the gang structure and channel the behavior
          of its members into more constructive activities

9. Research studies have demonstrated that the social health   9.___
   of a community is directly related to the
       A. opportunities available to its residents
       B. effectiveness of the police in the community
       C. number of social agencies located in the community
       D. influence of community organizations and groups

10. Because of the complexity of interacting forces contri-   10.___
    buting to the problems of the delinquent, the gang, and
    the community, the youth worker's efforts frequently meet
    with failure.
    It is, therefore, IMPORTANT for the supervisor to help
    his workers to concentrate their efforts with anti-social
    youth on
       A. attaining appropriate and often reasonably low levels
          of improvement
       B. helping mainly those group members who are most
          likely to profit from his attention
       C. protecting the community from the youths' destruc-
          tive and anti-social acts
       D. referring the most seriously disturbed youths to
          agencies staffed by psychiatric professionals

11. The PRIMARY concern of the youth worker who uses the group 11.___
    work approach with small gang groups would be the
       A. interrelationship of group members with each other,
          with their peers and with adults outside the group
       B. background of each group member in terms of his
          school, unemployment, and family problems
       C. nature and quality of the illegal activities engaged
          in by the members of the group
       D. attitudes expressed by local police agencies toward
          this type of approach with anti-social youths

12. For a youth worker to support the efforts of a conven-   12.____
tionally oriented subgroup of a gang to break away from
the rest of the group would GENERALLY be
   A. *undesirable*, chiefly because the two groups will
      probably engage in a gang fight if they separate
   B. *desirable*, if the behavior of the largest number of
      the group members is highly deviant and anti-social
   C. *undesirable*, chiefly because the conventionally
      oriented subgroup will no longer be able to prevent
      the highly deviant members from engaging in anti-
      social activities
   D. *desirable*, if the larger group is cohesive and the
      behavior of its members is somewhat constructive

13. A *vertical* group of gang members would be structured   13.____
according to
   A. turf   B. ethnicity
   C. age   D. leadership role

14. In terms of helping the group, which of the following   14.____
types of leadership would generally be considered MOST
acceptable for a youth worker to use with a loosely
structured, street-oriented group of youths?
   A. Laissez-faire   B. Manipulative
   C. Democratic   D. Autocratic

15. According to Richard A. Cloward and Lloyd E. Ohlin, in   15.____
DELINQUENCY AND OPPORTUNITY, members of a retreatist
sub-culture
   A. retreat during rumbles with members of other gangs
   B. are mainly involved in the use of drugs
   C. do not become involved in anti-social activities
   D. seek status through violent activities

16. Medical specialists and other health and community offi-   16.____
cials have reported that the recent resurgence of youth
gangs and youth violence has been accompanied by a
   A. considerable increase in youthful drug addiction and
      criminal activity involving drugs
   B. marked decrease in illegitimate pregnancies and
      requests for abortions from *women's auxiliary* gang
      members
   C. considerable increase in alcoholism and related ill-
      nesses and emergencies involving ghetto youth
   D. marked decrease in overdose cases and other indica-
      tions of narcotics use

17. An inexperienced youth worker assigned to a large gang   17.____
group expresses concern to his supervisor about the possibility of gang conflict and doesn't know which of the
members should be kept under closest surveillance.
The supervisor should advise him that is is MOST important
to give closest surveillance to the
   A. president   B. war counselor
   C. core members   D. peripheral members

18. The author of an early classic text on street gangs in   18.___
    Chicago is
    A. K.H. Rogers   B. Irving Spergel
    C. F.M. Thrasher   D. R.K. Merton

19. The members of an anti-social street gang who should be   19.___
    the objects of the MOST serious concern to youth workers
    are those who characteristically
    A. show an inability to cope effectively with their own
       impulsive behavior
    B. behave in a friendly, over-solicitous and helpful
       manner
    C. act bossy and try to convince the worker to accede
       to their demands
    D. refuse to accept the worker's friendly overtures and
       offers of assistance

20. The special language used by members of adolescent street   20.___
    gangs typically reflects their roles as alienated youth
    in a delinquent subculture.
    The one of the following which is NOT a usual charac-
    teristic of their vocabulary is
    A. grandiosity
    B. identification with the underdog
    C. possession of values counter to the larger society
    D. denial of reality

21. Assume that it has been decided that the youth services   21.___
    agency will terminate services to the *Lightning Rods*, a
    gang group which has not been involved in *jitterbugging*
    for about two years. When the members, who have developed
    a strong attachment to their worker, learn that soon they
    will no longer have regular contact with him, they start
    to fight and become involved in other anti-social inci-
    dents again. As a result, the worker tells his supervisor
    that he believes he should continue his assignment with
    the group.
    The supervisor SHOULD advise the worker to
    A. continue his services and so inform the group
    B. reassure the group that he will be available if
       needed, even though he will not see them regularly
    C. disregard the recent incidents, since this is the
       group's way of seeking attention
    D. make a sharp break with the group, and meet with
       him in order to discuss his apprehension about
       losing contact with these youths

22. A supervisor has a new worker whose records indicate that   22.___
    he has potential for becoming an excellent staff member.
    However, when the supervisor observes the worker in the
    field, he notices that the worker frequently holds back
    and seems uncertain in handling his group. When the
    supervisor talks to the worker about this in private, the
    worker explains that he hesitates because he is *afraid
    of doing the wrong thing*.

The BEST way for the supervisor to help this worker is to
A. assign him to another group until he gets more experience
B. suggest to him that he would feel better if he had professional training
C. give him reassurance and as much guidance as he needs
D. go into the field with him to work with his youths so he can learn directly from him

23. Assume that, when a supervisor visits a gang group for the first time, the group reacts to the supervisor in an antagonistic and hostile manner.
It would be ADVISABLE for the supervisor to
A. stop visiting the group until he learns from their worker that they have a more positive attitude toward him
B. discuss the situation with the assigned worker and direct him to call the group to a meeting in the unit office
C. return to visit the group frequently, making friendly approaches until a better relationship is established
D. take the group on a bus trip to Bear Mountain without their worker in order to foster a better relationship

23.____

24. Assume that a consultant, who has been brought in to review programs in a youth services agency unit, tells the supervisor that he has found that several workers have spent program money for their own personal needs.
The supervisor should FIRST
A. recommend that the workers involved be brought up on charges
B. realize that the consultant's findings may be biased, and take no further action until he hears from central office
C. accept the consultant's findings, because the consultant has the ultimate responsibility
D. review his records and discuss the findings with his staff, in order to determine the facts for himself

24.____

25. In the course of a field visit to a youth services agency unit, a supervisor learns that a youth worker has been involved sexually with one of the *debs* in his assigned group.
Which of the following would be the MOST appropriate action for the supervisor to take?
A. Suspend the worker immediately
B. Allow the worker to continue with his assigned group until a hearing is arranged
C. Confront the worker with his knowledge of the situation and assign him to the office pending further investigation
D. Confer with the worker and explain that such an involvement will eventually adversely affect his relationship with the group

25.____

Questions 26-30.

DIRECTIONS: Questions 26 through 30 are based on the following
              example of a youth worker's incident report. The
              report consists of ten numbered sentences, some of
              which are not consistent with the principles of good
              report writing.

     (1) On the evening of February 24, James and Larry, two
members of the *Black Devils*, were entering with a bottle of wine
in their hands. (2) It was unusually good wine for these boys to
buy. (3) I told them to give me the bottle and they refused, and
added that they wouldn't let anyone *put them out*. (4) I told them
they were entitled to have a good time, but they could not do it
the way they wanted; there were certain rules they had to observe.
(5) At this point, James said he had seen me box at camp and
suggested that Larry not accept my offer. (6) Then I said firmly
that the 25 cent admission fee did not give them the authority to
tell me what to do. (7) I also told them that, if they thought I
would fight them over such a matter, they were sadly mistaken.
(8) I added, however, that we could go to the gym right now and
settle it another way if they wished. (9) Larry immediately said
that he was sorry, he had not understood the rules, and he did not
want his quarter back. (10) On the other hand, they would not give
up their bottle either, so they left the premises.

26. Only material that is relevant to the main thought of a   26.___
     report should be included.
     Which of the following sentences from the report contains
     material which is LEAST relevant to this report?
     Sentence
        A. 2   B. 3   C. 8   D. 9

27. A good report should be arranged in logical order.   27.___
     Which of the following sentences from the report does
     NOT appear in its proper sequence in the report?
     Sentence
        A. 3   B. 5   C. 7   D. 9

28. Reports should include all essential information.   28.___
     Of the following, the MOST important fact that is missing
     from this report is
        A. who was involved in the incident
        B. how the incident was resolved
        C. when the incident took place
        D. where the incident took place

29. The MOST serious of the following faults commonly found   29.___
     in explanatory reports is
        A. use of slang terms   B. excessive details
        C. personal bias   D. redundancy

30. In reviewing a report he has prepared to submit to his   30.___
    superiors, a supervisor finds that his paragraphs are a
    typewritten page long and decides to make some revisions.
    Of the following, the MOST important question he should
    ask about each paragraph is:
    A. Are the words too lengthy?
    B. Is the idea under discussion too abstract?
    C. Is more than one central thought being expressed?
    D. Are the sentences too long?

———

KEY (CORRECT ANSWERS)

1. A	11. A	21. B
2. D	12. B	22. C
3. B	13. C	23. C
4. A	14. C	24. D
5. A	15. B	25. C
6. B	16. D	26. A
7. D	17. C	27. B
8. C	18. C	28. D
9. A	19. A	29. C
10. A	20. B	30. C

———

TEST 2

DIRECTIONS: Each question or incomplete statement is followed by several suggested answers or completions. Select the one that BEST answers the question or completes the statement. *PRINT THE LETTER OF THE CORRECT ANSWER IN THE SPACE AT THE RIGHT.*

1. Of the following, the factor that is MOST critical and MOST likely to influence the success of the youth worker's handling of aggression by gang group members is the
   A. time and place of the aggressive acts by the group members
   B. timing of the worker's action to curb the aggression
   C. number of group members taking part in the aggressive action
   D. availability of resources to distract the gang group members

1.___

2. When the leadership of a gang is highly negative or delinquent in nature, it is considered ADVISABLE for a worker who has a positive relationship with the group to
   A. assist the group to shift leadership from the delinquency oriented to the more conventionally oriented members
   B. attempt to oust the deviant leaders from the group
   C. give special attention to programs for the conventionally oriented members
   D. report the highly deviant leaders to the authorities in order to destroy their influence with the group

2.___

3. Of the following, the MOST important function of the central communications system in an area-based youth services unit is to permit the supervisor to
   A. learn where workers are in the field, and advise or direct them as to the most appropriate way of handling an emergency
   B. relay important information about unit activities and programs to higher-level personnel in the central office
   C. inform the community of the activities of the agency and its achievements in curbing delinquent behavior of neighborhood youth
   D. relay information about policies and procedures as well as routine matters to staff based in the field

3.___

4. Experts have criticized the use of the Glueck Juvenile Delinquency Prediction Table MAINLY because
   A. a child's personality changes during the various stages of growth
   B. statistics are irrelevant when applied to individuals
   C. personnel who use it may not be properly trained
   D. school personnel may not be objective with children identified as potentially delinquent

4.___

5. Under the present organization of the youth services   5.___
    agency, the basic unit of service is the
        A. central office
        B. technical assistance unit
        C. community planning district
        D. community board

6. The function of the *outreach* staff of the youth services   6.___
    agency is to
        A. provide professional casework services and in-service
           training to unit staff involved in referrals
        B. identify youths in the community with severe behavi-
           oral and psychological problems and refer them for
           professional help
        C. make contacts with community groups and agencies in
           order to help them administer their own programs
        D. provide youth with opportunities to take part in
           community planning and make suggestions for their
           own programs

7. A youth worker who wants to find out whether a youth in   7.___
    his group and his family are registered with other social
    and health agencies could get this information from the
        A. Community Service Society
        B. Social Service Exchange
        C. Contributors Information Bureau
        D. Council of Voluntary Agencies

8. Assume that the only guidelines used by a youth services   8.___
    agency staff member assigned to evaluate a contract agency
    were the contract agency's standards for administration,
    supervision, and programming.
    Of the following, the MOST important guideline omitted by
    the evaluator relates to the contract agency's
        A. lower-level staff   B. physical facilities
        C. board of directors   D. other funding resources

9. The MOST important purpose of social program evaluation   9.___
    as it is carried out in the youth services agency is to
        A. justify current program operations
        B. provide an objective basis for reductions in program
           funding
        C. introduce youth services agency personnel to profes-
           sionals in contract agencies
        D. provide an objective basis for decision-making on
           programs which will provide effective services to
           youth

10. The one of the following which is NOT usually included as   10.___
    part of the consultation services provided by the youth
    services agency staff member assigned to evaluate a
    contract agency is giving
        A. opinion and advice on program content
        B. information on resources in the youth services agency
           and the community
        C. help with the formulation of program proposals
        D. in-service training to agency staff

Questions 11-15.

DIRECTIONS: Questions 11 through 15 are to be answered SOLELY on
              the basis of the following passage.

In an attempt to describe what is meant by a delinquent subculture, let us look at some delinquent activities. We usually
assume that when people steal things, they steal because they want
them to eat or wear or otherwise use them; or because they can sell
them; or even - if we are given to a psychoanalytic turn of mind -
because on some deep symbolic level the things stolen substitute or
stand for something unconsciously desired but forbidden. However,
most delinquent gang stealing has no such utilitarian motivation at
all. Even where the value of the object stolen is itself a motivating consideration, the stolen sweets are often sweeter than those
acquired by more legitimate and prosaic means. In homelier language,
stealing *for the hell of it* and apart from considerations of gain
and profit is a valued activity to which attaches glory, prowess,
and profound satisfaction.

Similarly, many other delinquent activities are motivated mainly
by an enjoyment in the distress of others and by a hostility toward
non-gang peers as well as adults. Apart from the more dramatic
manifestations in the form of gang wars, there is keen delight in
terrorizing *good* children and in driving them from playgrounds and
gyms for which the gang itself may have little use. The same spirit
is evident in playing hooky and in misbehavior in school. The
teacher and her rules are not merely to be evaded. They are to be
flouted.

All this suggests that the delinquent subculture is not only a
set of rules, a design for living which is different from or indifferent to or even in conflict with the norms of the *respectable*
adult society. It actually takes its norms from the larger culture
but turns them upside down. The delinquent's conduct is right, by
the standards of his subculture, precisely because it is wrong by
the standards of the larger culture.

11. Of the following, the MOST suitable title for the above   11.____
     passage is
         A. DIFFERENT KINDS OF DELINQUENT SUBCULTURES
         B. DELINQUENT HOSTILITY TOWARD NON-GANG PEERS
         C. METHODS OF DELINQUENT STEALING
         D. DELINQUENT STANDARDS AS REVEALED BY THEIR ACTIVITIES

12. It may be inferred from the passage that MOST delinquent   12.____
     stealing is motivated by a
         A. need for food and clothing
         B. need for money to buy drugs
         C. desire for peer-approval
         D. symbolic identification of the thing stolen with
            hidden desires

13. The passage IMPLIES that an important reason why delin-   13.___
    quents play hooky and misbehave in school is that the
    teachers
    A. represent *respectable* society
    B. are boring
    C. have not taught them the values of the adult society
    D. are too demanding

14. In the passage, the author's attitude toward delinquents   14.___
    is
    A. critical   B. objective
    C. overly sympathetic   D. confused

15. According to the passage, which of the following state-   15.___
    ments is CORRECT?
    A. Delinquents derive no satisfaction from stealing.
    B. Delinquents are not hostile toward someone without
       a reason.
    C. The common motive of many delinquent activities is
       a desire to frustrate others.
    D. The delinquent subculture shares its standards with
       the *respectable* adult culture.

Questions 16-18.

DIRECTIONS: Questions 16 through 18 are to be answered SOLELY on
              the basis of the following paragraph.

A fundamental part of the youth worker's role is changing the
interaction patterns which already exist between the delinquent group
and the representatives of key institutions in the community, e.g.,
the policeman, teacher, social worker, employer, parent, and store-
keeper. This relationship, particularly its definitional character,
is a *two-way* proposition. The offending youth or group will usually
respond by fulfilling this prophecy. In the same way, the delinquent expects punishment or antagonistic treatment from officials
and other representatives of middle class society; in turn, the
adult concerned may act to fulfill the prophecy of the delinquent.
Stereotyped patterns of expectation, both of the delinquents and
those in contact with them, must be changed. The worker can be
instrumental in changing these patterns.

16. Of the following, the MOST suitable title for the para-   16.___
    graph is
    A. WAYS TO PREDICT JUVENILE DELINQUENCY
    B. THE YOUTH WORKER'S ROLE IN CREATING STEREOTYPES
    C. THE YOUTH WORKER'S ROLE IN CHANGING STEREOTYPED
       PATTERNS OF EXPECTATION
    D. THE DESIRABILITY OF INTERACTION PATTERNS

17. According to the paragraph, a youth who misbehaves and is 17.___
told by an agency worker that *his group is a menace to the community* would PROBABLY eventually respond by
    A. withdrawing into himself
    B. continuing to misbehave
    C. making a greater attempt to please
    D. acting indifferent

18. In this paragraph, the author's opinion about stereotypes 18.___
is that they are
    A. *useful*, primarily because they are usually accurate
    B. *useful*, primarily because they make a quick response easier
    C. *harmful*, primarily because the adult community will be less aware of delinquents as a group
    D. *harmful*, primarily because they influence behavior

Questions 19-20.

DIRECTIONS: Questions 19 and 20 are to be answered SOLELY on the basis of the following paragraph.

A drug-user does not completely retreat from society. While a new user, he must begin participation in some group of old users in order to secure access to a steady supply of drugs. In the process, his readiness to engage in drug use, which stems from his personality and the social structure, is reinforced by new patterns of associations and values. The more the individual is caught in this web of associations, the more likely it is that he will persist in drug use, for he has become incorporated into a subculture that exerts control over his behavior. However, it is also true that the resulting ties among addicts are not as strong as those among participants in criminal and conflict subcultures. Addiction is in many ways an individualistic adaptation, for the *kick* is essentially a private experience. The compelling need for the drug is also a divisive force, for it leads to intense competition among addicts for money. Forces of this kind thus limit the relative cohesion which can develop among users.

19. According to the paragraph, the MAIN reason why new drug 19.___
users associate with old users is a
    A. fear of the police   B. common hatred of society
    C. need to get drugs   D. dislike of being alone

20. According to the paragraph, which of the following state- 20.___
ments is INCORRECT?
    A. Drug users encourage each other to continue taking drugs.
    B. Gangs that use drugs are more cohesive than other delinquent gangs.
    C. A youth's desire to use drugs stems from his personality as well as the social structure.
    D. Addicts get no more of a *kick* from using drugs in a group than alone.

21. The MOST appropriate of the following methods for a super-   21.___
    visor to use FIRST in order to become knowledgeable about
    a gang group assigned to one of his workers is to
    A. work with the group on the worker's scheduled days
       off
    B. read the worker's recordings and discuss the group
       with the worker in supervisory conferences
    C. observe the worker in the field as he interacts with
       group members
    D. accompany the group on trips and other programmed
       activities

22. Assume that a supervisor has been assigned to take   22.___
    workers into a community which is in an uproar as a
    result of a recent outbreak of gang conflict during which
    a youth was killed. There were no youth services agency
    units or street workers in this community previously.
    The supervisor SHOULD approach this situation by
    A. calling a meeting with representatives of all the
       gang groups in order to assess the situation and
       discuss possible ways of curbing the conflicts
    B. contacting the police precinct for information about
       the hangouts of the gangs
    C. assigning workers to contact gang groups and urge
       them to move their activities out of the neighborhood
    D. meeting with the neighborhood leaders, staff of
       community organizations and other social agencies to
       discuss the magnitude of the problem and to mobilize
       resources

23. As a result of longstanding resentment between two gangs   23.___
    covered by a supervisor's unit, a popular youth who
    belonged to a third gang group was shot to death by
    accident.
    How should the supervisor handle this crisis?
    A. Immediately call a meeting of all the gang groups in
       the area to assess their feelings about the youth's
       death
    B. Mobilize unit workers to cover as many groups as
       possible, in order to be able to monitor their
       movements and plans
    C. Submit requests for buses to remove the two hostile
       groups from the area
    D. Request assistance from members of neighborhood
       auxiliary police in the area

24. In the course of a field visit, a supervisor learns for   24.___
    the first time that a worker has been discussing a weekend
    trip to Philadelphia with his assigned group when several
    youths in the group come up to him and ask for his deci-
    sion on the trip.
    The BEST course of action for the supervisor to take would
    be to tell the youths that

A. he approves of the trip, so that the youths will not be frustrated
B. he disapproves of the trip, so that the worker will learn to request approval before getting the youths excited about a trip
C. the worker did not discuss the trip with him, but that the worker will have to make the decision anyway
D. he is still considering the trip, and will evaluate it later on its own merits

25. It is frequently difficult for a supervisor to convince youth workers assigned to street gangs of the importance of recording.
While training his workers in proper recording methods, the supervisor should emphasize that, of the following, the MOST important purpose of recording is to
A. evaluate progress made by groups and individual members
B. determine the effectiveness of the agency as a whole
C. identify flaws in on-going programs
D. plan future programs

25.___

Questions 26-30.

DIRECTIONS: In Questions 26 through 30, choose the lettered word or expression which is closest to the meaning of the first word or expression, *as used most frequently by street-oriented youths and members of youth gangs.* Do not try to give the usually accepted or dictionary definition of the word or expression.

26. wig out
    A. shoplift clothes   B. engage in homosexuality
    C. feel shocked   D. refuse to use drugs

26.___

27. dipple
    A. cocaine user   B. former hippie
    C. unit of drugs   D. nervous junkie

27.___

28. flaky
    A. a little abnormal mentally
    B. nervy
    C. enjoyable
    D. beaten to a pulp

28.___

29. wag tail
    A. succeed   B. conform   C. fool   D. inform

29.___

30. dolphins
    A. amphetamines   B. suspicious pushers
    C. methadone pills   D. pimps

30.___

———

KEY (CORRECT ANSWERS)

1. B	11. D	21. B
2. A	12. C	22. D
3. A	13. A	23. B
4. D	14. B	24. D
5. C	15. C	25. A
6. B	16. C	26. C
7. B	17. B	27. B
8. A	18. D	28. A
9. D	19. C	29. B
10. D	20. B	30. C

EXAMINATION SECTION ✓

DIRECTIONS: Each question or incomplete statement is followed by several suggested answers or completions. Select the one that BEST answers the question or completes the statement. *PRINT THE LETTER OF THE CORRECT ANSWER IN THE SPACE AT THE RIGHT.*

1. A youth worker asks his supervisor what to do about his gang group whose members have informed him that they are planning to *go down* on another group for *jumping* one of their members on his way home from school.
It would be best for the supervisor to recommend that the worker should FIRST
   A. individually question the members of his group about the incident
   B. engage the group members in activities outside of the neighborhood
   C. arrange a mediation meeting involving both groups
   D. report the information to police to avoid further trouble

1.___

2. A youth worker tells his supervisor that the owner of a local bowling alley has asked him to bring his gang group over for recreation. A financial arrangement beneficial to the worker was suggested as part of the plan.
The supervisor should advise the worker to
   A. refuse the offer because he should avoid entanglements that might compromise the agency or his professional conduct
   B. refuse the offer because he should avoid contact with the business community
   C. accept the offer but refuse payment because he should utilize all resources offered to gang members
   D. accept the offer but refuse payment because he can use the situation to establish a relationship with a member of the business community

2.___

3. Assume that a youth worker who previously had important responsibilities complains to his supervisor about having to share periodic office coverage. This employee has been back for a few months after a serious illness and is not yet able to resume all of his previous responsibilities, but is well enough to function as a worker.
The BEST way for the supervisor to handle this complaint is to
   A. refer the problem to his area administrator because of the special nature of the case
   B. excuse the employee from office coverage
   C. suggest to the employee that he may be well enough to take on his previous responsibilities again
   D. tell the employee that office coverage must be shared by all workers in the unit

3.___

4. During a unit staff meeting, several youth workers raise
   objections to a certain youth services agency policy and
   make suggestions for revision of the policy that seem to
   the supervisor to have considerable merit.
   The MOST appropriate action for the supervisor to take
   would be to
   A. allow the workers to interpret the policy according
      to their suggestions, which relate to the needs of
      this neighborhood
   B. inform the workers that policy changes must be
      initiated and implemented by higher administrative
      personnel of the agency
   C. help the workers prepare a proposal outlining their
      suggestions to be submitted by the unit to higher
      administrative personnel
   D. report to his administrator that his workers object
      to the policy and that considerable revision is
      required

4.___

5. Which of the following methods available to the supervisor of youth workers is usually MOST effective in
   facilitating communication with his subordinates?
   A. Weekly staff meetings   B. Memoranda
   C. Unscheduled conferences   D. Workshops

5.___

6. Several youths who belong to a gang group come to the
   supervisor with a problem that should have been handled
   by their assigned youth worker. As they talk to the
   supervisor, the youths also make strong complaints about
   their worker.
   Of the following, it would be advisable for the supervisor to
   A. ignore the complaints at this time because it is
      risky to accept reports from gang members without
      further investigation
   B. report the incident to the area administrator and
      ask him to deal administratively with this worker
   C. review the worker's records and discuss the problem
      with him and the youths before taking further action
   D. have the worker transferred to another unit because
      he seems to be in danger of attack by these youths

6.___

7. Of the following, the factor that the supervisor should
   consider MOST important in evaluating a youth worker's
   performance is
   A. how frequently he asks for guidance
   B. his willingness to be helpful and cooperative
   C. his consistency in keeping his recording up to date
   D. his interest in his group members and his effective-
      ness in dealing with them

7.___

8. Assume that a citizens' group addresses a letter of   8.___
   commendation to a supervisor praising the youth workers
   on his staff for their extraordinary service in helping
   to deal with several emergencies involving youth in the
   area.
   Of the following, it would be advisable for the supervisor to FIRST
       A. send the letter to the director of field operations
       B. call in the staff member who was most helpful and
          commend him in private
       C. write a letter of thanks to the citizens' group
          in the name of his staff
      \D. share this commendation with his staff and his area
          administrator

9. A worker reports to his supervisor that one of his group   9.___
   members has begun to experiment with marijuana. The
   worker feels uneasy about handling the situation and asks
   for guidance.
   The supervisor should advise the worker to
       A. ignore the situation since most youths experiment
          with marijuana
       B. refer the youth to a drug prevention program
      √C. confront the youth and discuss the situation with
          him
       D. discuss the situation with the youth's parents

10. In a supervisory conference, a worker asks for guidance   10.___
    about how to handle the problem of a 22-year-old dropout
    who wants to return to school in the daytime to obtain
    a high school diploma so that he can apply to a community
    college. The worker has contacted the youth's former
    school, but the principal refuses to take the youth back
    because of his age.
    Of the following, the supervisor's BEST approach would
    be to advise the worker to
        A. contact the district school superintendent's office
           and request an exception in the case of this youth
        B. tell the youth's parents to submit an appeal to the
           Board of Education
        C. refer the youth to a vocational training program
           instead
       √D. urge the youth to attend evening high school and
           work during the day

11. A youth worker tells his superior he has definite   11.___
    evidence that one of his group members is *dealing*, but
    hesitates to identify the youth because he does not
    want to violate the principle of confidentiality.
    The supervisor should
        A. give the worker a direct order to identify the
           youth and take disciplinary action if the worker
           refuses
        B. reassign this worker to another group since he seems
           to be over-identifying with this youth

√ C. discuss with the worker the reasons for reporting
    illegal acts and clarify agency policy and the need
    to enforce it
   D. visit and observe the group himself in order to
    identify the youth who is *dealing*

12. During his review of workers' recordings, a supervisor
    finds that one of his workers refers most youths who
    ask him about employment to a job placement agency after
    interviewing them only once.
    Of the following, the BEST advice the supervisor can give
    this worker is:
    A. Workers should try to find suitable openings in the
       neighborhood before referring youths to a job place-
       ment agency
    B. As a rule, a worker should interview youths seeking
       employment more than once in order to determine
       their needs and prepare them before referring them
       to an outside agency
    C. The youths are probably asking the worker to help
       them find employment in order to get attention and
       emotional support and are not really ready to get
       jobs
    D. Workers should make every effort to convince youths
       to go back to school and refer them for jobs only
       as a last resort

12.___

13. In a discussion with her supervisor about one of her
    group members, a female youth worker reports that she
    is planning to encourage 18-year-old Maria, who was
    born in Puerto Rico and is employed, to leave home
    because her father is very domineering.
    It would be appropriate for the supervisor to
    A. support the worker because an 18-year-old girl who
       has a job needs to be more independent
    B. advise the worker not to encourage Maria to leave
       home at this time and refer Maria's father to a
       casework agency
    C. advise the worker not to encourage Maria to leave
       home and try to help Maria's mother to assert a
       more active role
    D. determine whether the worker realizes that Maria's
       father may be assuming the patriarchal role which
       would be traditional for him

13.___

14. A youth worker tells his supervisor that he feels that
    he does not have enough leeway in serving his group and
    must rigidly follow too many regulations and procedures.
    Of the following, the BEST way for the supervisor to
    help this worker is to
    A. tell him that as long as he uses good judgment he
       need not worry about regulations and procedures
    B. compliment the worker whenever he interprets
       regulations and procedures less rigidly

14.___

    C. ask him for program suggestions and assure him that his ideas will be considered

    D. give him additional authority and responsibility

15. A supervisor learns that a youth worker with considerable experience has recently been acting hostile to his group and has not been providing services requested by the members.
The supervisor's FIRST action should be to discuss this behavior with the worker and

    A. suggest that he consult with a therapist about his unconscious motives

    B. try to help him understand why he is acting hostile

    C. suggest to him that he may not like the group

    D. point out that the group may not react to the worker's hostility

15.___

16. A youth worker asks his supervisor for guidance about a 15-year-old youth who had been one of the most constructive members of his group, but has recently been getting into trouble. The youth's father died ten years ago, and his mother has just remarried.
The supervisor should help the worker to realize that the youth

    A. is probably going through a crisis and should be given special attention

    B. probably dislikes his stepfather and is misbehaving in the hope of being placed away from home

    C. will stop misbehaving if his present conduct is not taken too seriously

    D. should be warned that further misbehavior must be reported to his stepfather

16.___

17. During a weekly conference with his supervisor, a worker reports that a youth in his group has told him that his father is *messing around* with his 13-year-old sister. When the sister confided in the youth, she said that the father threatened to kill her if she told anyone that he was having sex with her, and the youth is frightened.
The supervisor should FIRST

    A. call the father into his office on the pretext of discussing the youth's problems in order to assess the situation

    B. have the worker report the situation to the local juvenile aid police officer

    C. have the worker report the situation immediately to the local child protective services unit of the Bureau of Child Welfare

    D. call the sister into the office in order to obtain the facts for himself

17.___

18. A youth worker who has a friend in central office is
    continually spreading rumors that he claims to have
    heard from his *connections downtown*. These rumors
    often sound true and are upsetting to staff.
    The MOST advisable action for the supervisor of this
    unit to take at this point would be to
    - A. tell his staff to disregard the stories spread by
      this worker
    - B. report the worker to the director of field operations
      and request that he be reprimanded for his behavior
    - C. arrange the worker's assignments so that he will
      have nothing more to do with central office
    - D. tell the worker privately that his rumors are
      creating a morale problem and he must stop spreading
      them at once

18.___

19. A supervisor of a youth services unit has interviewed
    the father of an 18-year-old youth who says that the boy
    has been stealing, moody, and *hangs around with a bunch
    of no-good junkies*. The supervisor has reason to
    believe that the boy is experimenting with hard drugs,
    but the father does not seem to be able to cope with
    this because of his fears and his pride in the family.
    When the supervisor assigns a worker to this case,
    it would be appropriate for him to tell the worker to
    start out by
    - A. telling the father that the boy is on hard drugs
      and should be in treatment
    - B. suggesting to the father to have the boy put under
      observation by the youth division of the police
      department
    - C. talking with the father about widespread drug use
      and narcotic addiction among middle-class youth
      in order to relieve him of his guilt
    - D. assuring the father that confidentiality will be
      upheld and that he should feel free to discuss his
      fears

19.___

20. A supervisor finds it necessary to intervene in a heated
    argument between two of his workers. One worker, who
    comes from a middle class background, insists that drug
    abuse is due mainly to psychological problems, while
    the other worker, who was brought up in the ghetto,
    insists that drug abuse is due to the pressures of *the
    street*.
    The BEST way for the supervisor to handle this dispute
    would be to
    - A. assign the middle-class worker to the office since
      he is probably having difficulty working in the
      street
    - B. tell the workers to *cool it* and separate them in
      their assignments in the field
    - C. help the workers to see that both are partly right
      and could probably learn from each other if they
      could manage to have a calm discussion

20.___

  D. give both workers reliable literature on drug abuse
    so that they will get the facts in proper perspec-
    tive

Questions 21-30.

DIRECTIONS: In Questions 21 through 30, choose the lettered word or
       expression which is CLOSEST to the meaning of the first
       word or expression, *as used most frequently by street-
       oriented youths and members of youth gangs.* Do not try
       to give the usually accepted or dictionary definition
       of the word or expression.

21. *dyke*   21.___
   A. *crack* package   B. packet of narcotics
   C. opium addict   D. female homosexual

22. *burned out*   22.___
   A. kicked the habit   B. took an overdose
   C. pulled a robbery   D. challenged a rival gang

23. *drop acid*   23.___
   A. buy LSD   B. take LSD
   C. stay off LSD   D. sell LSD

24. *juicehead*   24.___
   A. homosexual   B. natural food faddist
   C. *ice* user   D. alcoholic

25. *threads*   25.___
   A. popped veins   B. police connections
   C. complications   D. clothes

26. *out of sight*   26.___
   A. conventional   B. superb
   C. informed   D. forbidden

27. *hairy*   27.___
   A. difficult   B. smart
   C. torn into shreds   D. mentally disturbed

28. *blowing snow*   28.___
   A. cheating   B. giving up
   C. sniffing cocaine   D. keeping secret

29. *feed your head*   29.___
   A. steal food   B. fall asleep
   C. act crazy   D. take drugs

30. *racked up*   30.___
   A. taken an overdose   B. drunk
   C. upset   D. hiding from the police

KEY (CORRECT ANSWERS)

1. A	11. C	21. D
2. A	12. B	22. A
3. D	13. D	23. B
4. C	14. C	24. D
5. A	15. B	25. D
6. C	16. A	26. B
7. D	17. C	27. A
8. D	18. D	28. C
9. C	19. D	29. D
10. D	20. C	30. C

TEST 2

DIRECTIONS: Each question or incomplete statement is followed by several suggested answers or completions. Select the one that BEST answers the question or completes the statement. *PRINT THE LETTER OF THE CORRECT ANSWER IN THE SPACE AT THE RIGHT.*

1. A youth comes running into the unit office and reports that a Black youth has been killed in a fight between Black and Puerto Rican gang members and that Black adults in the community are in an uproar and are threatening violence against Puerto Ricans.
   Of the following, the supervisor should FIRST
   A. call Black and Puerto Rican adult community leaders into his office in order to enlist their help in preventing further violence
   B. assign as many Black and Puerto Rican workers as possible to the respective gang groups in an attempt to *cool it*
   C. get immediate field reports from workers in the affected areas in order to get an accurate picture of the situation
   D. call Black and Puerto Rican gang leaders into his office for a mediation meeting

   1.___

2. The *Social Seven*, a gang group, have not had a gang fight for the past 16 months, and most of the members have not been involved in any other anti-social incidents recently. The assigned worker suggests termination of services to this group and asks his supervisor to be reassigned to the *Spanish Lads*, a real *down* group.
   The appropriate action for the supervisor to take at this point would be to
   A. reassign the worker since the *Social Seven* are not likely to get into trouble at this stage
   B. keep the worker with the *Social Seven* since a gang group's behavior is unpredictable
   C. set up meetings with the worker to discuss the pros and cons of termination of services to the *Social Seven*
   D. advise the worker to continue working with the *Social Seven* but to make less contact with them and drift away gradually

   2.___

3. A 15-year-old youth who attends high school comes into the office at a time when he should be on his way to school and asks for help in finding a part-time job after school.
   The BEST way for the worker to handle this situation is to
   A. interview the youth about a job so that he does not waste the day
   B. refuse to interview the youth at the time and advise him to go to school and return at the end of the day

   3.___

C. interview the youth and determine his reasons for
   wanting a job
D. phone the youth's parents and advise them that the
   youth is out of school that day

4. A worker has had considerable discussion with a youth   4.___
   about his problems and decides that he should be referred
   to another agency for special treatment.
   Which of the following would be the MOST appropriate way
   for the worker to handle the referral?
   A. Send the youth to the agency with a brief note since
      the youth can best explain his problems.
   B. Phone the intake worker of the agency to discuss the
      youth's case and have the agency make the initial
      contact with the youth.
   C. Talk to the youth about the referral process before
      and after making contact and discussing the youth's
      case with a representative of the agency.
   D. Offer the youth a choice of several suitable agencies
      and have him make the initial contact.

5. After preparing a youth for referral to a treatment   5.___
   center, a youth worker should usually maintain close
   contact with both the youth and his therapist.
   This continued contact is important MAINLY because the
   A. worker will be able to take the supportive role
      needed to keep the youth in treatment
   B. youth will be able to get a more realistic picture
      of the treatment process
   C. worker will have a chance to get first-hand know-
      ledge about the treatment process
   D. therapist will have a chance to meet the worker

6. In order to make suitable referrals and use community   6.___
   agencies to the greatest extent possible, it is MOST
   important for the youth worker to know
   A. what services the agencies have to offer
   B. the locations of the central offices of the agencies
   C. how the agencies are funded
   D. prominent staff members of the agencies

7. A supervisor who has been working with his staff to   7.___
   implement a job program for youths in his area drafts
   a program proposal to submit to the director of field
   operations. The items covered in the proposal are
   resources, population to be served, priorities, role of
   the agency, participation of the community in the program,
   staff needs, and budget needs.
   Of the following, a KEY factor which has been OMITTED is
   A. names of interested community leaders
   B. documentation of need for the program
   C. approval of the unit staff
   D. approval of the community

8. A worker comes to his supervisor for help in handling the   8.___
   problem of a 14-year-old youth who is talking about *splitting* from home. The worker has developed a close relationship with this youth and his family and does not consider the situation to be serious enough to justify the youth's desire to leave home.
   It would be advisable for the supervisor to
   A. help the worker to see that he is over-identifying with the youth and his family and should become less involved
   B. have the worker contact the youth division in the local precinct because experience indicates that this youth will probably run away from home
   C. discuss with the worker some specific ways to help this youth by *talking it out* with him and his parents
   D. help the worker to see that this is a big *put on* by the youth to get attention

9. An inexperienced female youth worker in a supervisor's   9.___
   unit has been working with a group of 13- to 15-year-old girls. The worker's records indicate that whenever the girls start talking about sex, having babies, and abortions, the worker becomes very formal and does her best to get them to change the subject.
   The supervisor should
   A. encourage the worker to continue to act as an authority figure with the girls and to avoid talking about sex with them
   B. realize that the worker has a hang-up about sex and is unlikely to be able to handle girls with precocious sexual knowledge and behavior
   C. tell the worker that she is being too hard on these girls and will have a better relationship with them if she can talk about sex on their level
   D. realize that the girls may be *testing* the worker and that she may not be confident enough to handle this yet and needs the supervisor's help and support

10. A youth worker in a supervisor's unit is unusually out-   10.___
    spoken and assertive and often gets into heated discussions with colleagues in the unit and youth workers from other agencies over services the worker feels are needed by his group.
    The BEST way for the supervisor to attempt to resolve this problem is to
    A. help the other workers in the unit to stay *cool* when this worker gets excited about his group's unmet needs
    B. have the worker transferred to another unit
    C. help the worker to become more diplomatic with colleagues and representatives of outside agencies
    D. encourage the worker to keep being assertive because it is the only way to get results

11. A recently arrived Puerto Rican youth who speaks no   11.___
    English comes to a youth services agency office asking
    for help in finding employment.
    The supervisor's FIRST step should be to
        A. refer the youth to an employment agency where Spanish
           is spoken
        B. refer the youth to a program for learning English
           as a second language
        C. assign a Spanish-speaking worker to interview the
           youth and evaluate his needs
        D. assign the youth to a worker and suggest that a
           job be developed for the youth where English will
           not be needed

12. As a result of several meetings held with neighborhood   12.___
    residents by a youth worker, the community is becoming
    more interested in problems of local youths. After
    several months, the community group makes a request
    through the worker for help from the youth services
    agency in establishing a small, locally-run youth
    center.
    It would be BEST for the youth worker's supervisor to
        A. suggest to the worker that the program plan may be
           premature
        B. tell the worker to advise the community group to
           raise funds for the center in the neighborhood
        C. have the worker help the group to prepare their
           program request for submission to higher levels in
           the agency
        D. submit the community's plan to the program planning
           committee

13. Of the following, the CHIEF cause of death among people   13.___
    between 15-25 years of age is
        A. lead poisoning   B. drug abuse
        C. suicide   D. malnutrition

14. Some psychiatrists and psychologists have a low opinion   14.___
    of the street club worker's function and his value in
    changing the behavior of anti-social youths.
    Of the following, the MOST serious consequence of such
    an attitude is that it may
        A. cause street club workers to resent other profes-
           sionals
        B. discourage street club workers from referring youths
           to psychologists and psychiatrists
        C. result in transference of this negative attitude
           about street club workers to their group members
        D. make it difficult for street club workers to obtain
           professional training

15. Assume that the unit supervisor observes that a youth   15.___
who is waiting in the office for his first interview
with a worker is nervous, sweating, yawning, and constantly blowing his nose.
It would be important for the supervisor to
   A. discuss his observations and possible reasons for
the youth's behavior with the worker who interviews
him
   B. call the youth into his office for a brief talk in
order to observe him more closely
   C. greet the youth casually and try to put him at ease
before the interview
   D. discuss the youth's behavior with him at length
before he is interviewed by the worker

16. Assume that a group of mothers comes to the local youth   16.___
services agency office with the complaint that their
pre-adolescent children are in danger of getting into
trouble because there are very few recreational facilities available for them in the neighborhood. They ask
the supervisor for his help in developing more recreational resources.
Of the following, the MOST appropriate action for the
supervisor to take FIRST would be to
   A. refer the matter to the department of recreation
   B. discuss the request with administrative officials
of the youth services agency
   C. discuss the situation with workers assigned in the
neighborhood since they should have pertinent
information about recreational facilities
   D. invite mothers to a meeting with other interested
community people in an effort to properly identify
the problem

17. The president of the neighborhood block association   17.___
invites the supervisor of the local youth services
agency unit for the first time to a meeting called to
discuss community problems caused by the anti-social
behavior of gang youth in the area.
The supervisor should welcome the opportunity to attend
this meeting MAINLY because it would enable him to
   A. gain some insight into the feelings of neighborhood
adults about gang youths and explain to them how
agency workers relate to anti-social youths
   B. gain additional insight into the gang members'
feelings and concerns about neighborhood adults
   C. assure members of the block association that the
youth services agency is making substantial progress
in curbing anti-social behavior of local youth
   D. gather specific complaints from neighborhood adults
about the behavior of individual youths so that he
can assign workers to give additional attention to
curbing their anti-social acts

18. Assume that a youth worker newly assigned to a gang
    group becomes friendly with Dano, a member of the group,
    and wants Dano to help him make his first contacts with
    the other members.
    Before proceeding further, it is important for the
    worker to
    A. inform Dano that he has been assigned to the area
       by the youth services agency to work with the group
    B. question Dano about the group without identifying
       himself as a representative of the youth services
       agency
    C. talk about sports and other matters that would
       interest Dano and give no indication that he is
       a youth worker assigned to the group
    D. ask Dano to arrange for the worker to meet with
       the group as a whole

18.____

19. Assume that a youth worker recently assigned to a gang
    group has been able to make friends with a few of the
    members individually. However, the more powerful mem-
    bers of the group seem to resent his presence in the
    area.
    At this point, the worker should
    A. continue to relate to the individual members of the
       group
    B. try to convince the leader of the group that he can
       do a lot for them
    C. leave the area because he may be in danger of physi-
       cal attack by the hostile members
    D. invite the entire group to go out with him for
       refreshments

19.____

20. A youth worker reports to his assigned area and is told
    by one of his gang group members that the group is angry
    with him and wants him to leave the neighborhood.
    The worker can BEST approach this situation by
    A. locating the other members and trying to find out
       what their attitude is toward him
    B. leaving the neighborhood for the day in the hope
       that the situation will resolve itself
    C. asking his supervisor for temporary reassignment to
       another group until the hostile members *cool off*
    D. arranging an informal gathering with refreshments
       and inviting the hostile members

20.____

21. Several workers present their supervisor with excellent
    proposals for programs with their assigned groups. How-
    ever, the supervisor finds that staff and budget
    resources are far from adequate to implement these pro-
    grams as planned by the workers.
    Of the following, it would usually be advisable for the
    supervisor to
    A. request additional funds to carry out the programs
    B. ask the workers to review the programs and resubmit
       them after making revisions wherever possible to
       reduce staff and funding requirements

21.____

    C. approve the programs on a priority basis, implement-
       ing first those planned for the groups with the most
       serious problems
    D. ask his administrator for guidance on how to allocate
       staff and funds

22. A supervisor has been directed by his area administrator 22.___
to assign one of his workers to a special task to be
completed within a month and gives the assignment to a
worker whom he considers most capable of doing the job.
The worker seems hesitant but accepts the assignment
without comment, even though he is told that he will be
relieved of some of his regular work. However, when the
supervisor checks on the worker's progress a week later,
he finds that he has not started to work on the assignment.
The BEST action for the supervisor to take is to
    A. give part of the assignment to another worker since
       it must be completed to meet the deadline
    B. report the worker to the area administrator for
       insubordination
    C. remind the worker about the assignment and assure
       him of your confidence that he will complete it on
       time
    D. reassign the entire task to another worker

23. Assume that the supervisor of a youth services agency 23.___
unit makes demands upon a new worker which are beyond
the worker's present capabilities.
Of the following, the MOST probable result of the supervisor's actions would be to
    A. give the worker an incentive to learn at a faster
       pace
    B. undermine the worker's confidence and inhibit him
       from fulfilling his present capabilities
    C. demonstrate the need for formal in-service training
       before a new worker is assigned to a unit
    D. encourage the worker to seek professional training
       in order to improve his performance

24. A worker reports to his supervisor that one of the sub- 24.___
groups in a youth council is led by a youth who has many
constructive ideas but whose contribution is limited
because of his rivalry with the elected president of the
council.
Of the following, the supervisor should advise the
worker to
    A. allow the youths to settle this problem without out-
       side assistance
    B. tell the leader of the sub-group to withhold his
       ideas until he becomes an elected officer
    C. attempt to curb the rivalry so that the leader of
       the sub-group can get his ideas across
    D. appoint the leader of the sub-group to the executive
       board of the council

25. A worker tells his supervisor that he is troubled because 25.____
the youths in his group are continually asking him
personal questions, and he does not know how to answer
them.
Of the following, it would be BEST for the supervisor to
advise the worker to
   A. try to find out why the youths are asking these
      questions
   B. point out to the youths that it would not be pro-
      fessional to answer personal questions
   C. try to give a brief, truthful answer and immediately
      redirect the youths to their own problems
   D. tell the youths everything they want to know in
      order to foster a friendly relationship

26. The supervisor should advise new staff members that, in 26.____
working with adolescent groups, it is important for the
worker to give guidance
   A. at every opportunity
   B. only when the members ask for it
   C. without becoming the group leader himself
   D. to a greater extent to the less aggressive members

27. A youth worker reports to his supervisor that the 27.____
behavior of the youths in his group is fairly orderly
while he is with them, but that roughhousing breaks out
as soon as he leaves them.
Of the following, the MOST reasonable explanation for
this change in their behavior is that
   A. the worker is not exercising enough control
   B. this is the typical behavior pattern of anti-social
      youth
   C. the worker is probably too strict and *tight* with
      them
   D. the youths dislike the worker and resent his presence

28. Most adolescents hesitate to risk disapproval by showing 28.____
their fears and anxieties. However, repressing these
fears and anxieties may lead to more serious psychological problems.
The one of the following which would be the MOST appropriate method for a youth worker to use in order to
help his group overcome their fears and anxieties would
be to schedule
   A. regular sessions during which the members are
      encouraged to discuss their fears and anxieties
   B. activities that are not likely to produce fears
      and anxieties
   C. programs that give special emphasis to wrestling,
      boxing, and competitive sports
   D. talks by professionals on typical adolescent fears
      and anxieties

29. In attempting to achieve constructive goals by means of   29.___
    programs, it is particularly important for the youth
    worker to be aware that delinquent youths
      A. are usually more interested in activities that take
         them away from their immediate neighborhood
      B. tend to *act out* feelings and express themselves by
         means of activity rather than verbal exchange
      C. tend to participate more actively if the youth
         worker takes a passive role while the program is in
         progress
      D. are best suited to activities that require consider-
         able sharing and integration of effort

30. According to observers of present-day gang groups, the   30.___
    gang leaders often choose a member who is a minor to
    commit a crime for the group as a whole.
    The MOST plausible reason why the gang would make such
    a choice is that a minor is
      A. usually stereotyped by the police
      B. less likely to receive a long prison sentence
      C. more likely to be released on his own recognizance
      D. easier to hide from the police

KEY (CORRECT ANSWERS)

1. C	11. C	21. B
2. C	12. C	22. C
3. B	13. B	23. B
4. C	14. B	24. C
5. A	15. A	25. C
6. A	16. D	26. C
7. B	17. A	27. C
8. C	18. A	28. A
9. D	19. A	29. B
10. C	20. A	30. B

EXAMINATION SECTION
TEST 1

DIRECTIONS: Each question or incomplete statement is followed by several suggested answers or completions. Select the one that BEST answers the question or completes the statement. *PRINT THE LETTER OF THE CORRECT ANSWER IN THE SPACE AT THE RIGHT.*

1. The one of the following which CORRECTLY describes the general characteristics of a typical street gang is a
    A. loosely federated group of youths, who take part in occasional delinquent acts as well as social and recreational activities
    B. closely-attached clique of friends, who require approval of each new member by a committee of older members
    C. highly unstructured youth group with at least 100 members and several elected officers
    D. group composed of no more than 10 or 12 close friends who have all grown up on the same street

1.____

2. Of the following, a SIGNIFICANT difference between present-day youth gangs and the youth gangs of the 1950's is that gang members today
    A. are talking about solving such problems as housing, jobs, and getting off welfare
    B. are generally younger and less sophisticated
    C. use a language of their own
    D. are less likely to have criminal records

2.____

3. Statistics indicate that more delinquent acts are committed by youth who come from families of low socio-economic status than by middle- or upper-class youth. The one of the following which is GENERALLY considered to be an important reason for these statistics is that
    A. middle- and upper-class youth are protected by their parents' influence and are generally treated more leniently by police
    B. youth of lower socioeconomic status usually have weaker characters
    C. behavior considered to be a crime by lower-class families is not considered criminal by middle-class families
    D. middle- and upper-class youth are clever in concealing their illegal acts

3.____

4. Members of a minority group which experiences discrimination by a dominant group USUALLY react by
    A. seeking security by establishing social relationships with the dominant group
    B. choosing its leaders from the dominant group

4.____

C. becoming more closely unified as a reaction to such
   discrimination
D. becoming disorganized as individual members seek
   acceptance from the dominant group

5. Assume that, as a result of several recent gang killings,   5.___
   the newspapers have been editorializing about the evils
   of youth gangs, demanding that the police arrest gang
   leaders and members of street corner youth groups.
   Which of the following would be the MOST advisable action
   for the administration of a youth services agency to take
   in an attempt to relieve tension created by these newspaper articles?
   A. Order staff to work more intensively with their
      assigned groups and program them in activities out-
      side of their neighborhoods
   B. Have the public relations office invite newsmen to
      tour the neighborhoods, describing the agency's work
      with gangs and the constructive aspects of group
      relationships
   C. Instruct workers to talk to members of youth gangs
      and order them not to *hang out* on street corners
   D. Instruct workers to talk to the police and describe
      to them the youth services agency's constructive
      work with youth groups

6. Research has shown that the MAJOR form of delinquency   6.___
   among street-oriented girls' gangs is
   A. petty theft, such as shoplifting
   B. sexual misbehavior, including promiscuity and
      prostitution
   C. helping boys' gangs in criminal activities
   D. violent attacks on other girls, or street muggings

7. Recent studies indicate that MOST youth gangs in low-   7.___
   income neighborhoods have
   A. a stable group of all-male members
   B. female members who take more passive roles than the
      male members
   C. an approximately equal number of male and female
      members
   D. definite goals which are formulated by the male
      members

8. A hospital would probably be a more favorable setting   8.___
   than a commercial laundry for a work project for disad-
   vantaged youths, no matter what kind of work they are
   assigned to do, MAINLY because a hospital would
   A. be more likely to offer steady employment and fringe
      benefits
   B. expose youths with delinquent tendencies to fewer
      temptations
   C. give the youths more opportunity to become acquainted
      with adults who work at higher occupational levels
   D. be more likely to tolerate unacceptable behavior on
      the job

9. A suggestion has been made that the parents of delinquent 9.___
   youths, rather than the youths themselves, be brought into
   court for trial.
   Of the following, the MOST forceful argument against this
   suggestion is that
      A. court action against the parents will lower their
         prestige in the eyes of their children
      B. parents cannot be considered responsible for the
         delinquent acts of their children
      C. court action against the parents will not cause the
         children to feel guilty for their acts
      D. juvenile delinquents cannot be helped to change their
         behavior unless they are made to feel fully respon-
         sible for their acts

10. Of the following, the MAIN reason why a worker has an 10.___
    important part to play in encouraging street-oriented
    youths to participate in education-work-training programs
    is that
       A. the worker is best qualified to provide needed infor-
          mation on available employment
       B. schools and other organizations might not be willing
          to refer youths with histories of delinquent behavior
          to these programs
       C. street-oriented youths are not likely to be reached
          through schools and other organizations which usually
          make referrals to such programs
       D. the worker may be the only person who could provide
          prospective employers with objective information
          about the youths

11. Of the following, the MAIN reason why membership in a 11.___
    peer group is of great importance to adolescents is that
    the peer group provides
       A. ways to achieve a meaningful social identity
       B. opportunity to cover up criminal activity
       C. protection from the police
       D. opportunity to *fight the system*

12. In general, it has been found that the lower the socio- 12.___
    economic level of its neighborhood, the more likely a
    gang is to
       A. become involved in anti-social and violent activity
       B. benefit from participation in team sports
       C. have several members hung up on heroin
       D. suspect the worker to be a police informer

13. Research studies show that commitment of delinquent youth 13.___
    to correctional institutions, juvenile homes, training
    schools, and other similar facilities has GENERALLY led to
       A. rehabilitation of the individual offender
       B. a high rate of return to these institutions
       C. a temporary decrease in delinquent behavior by fellow
          gang members
       D. an overall reduction in crime in the community

14. With regard to youthful offenders, statistics on arrests   14.___
    and court commitments of youth tend to
    A. exaggerate the relative seriousness of crimes com-
       mitted by juveniles
    B. give an accurate picture of the amount of juvenile
       delinquency
    C. exaggerate the total amount of juvenile delinquency
    ✓D. underestimate the total amount of juvenile delinquency

15. It is generally considered desirable for the worker to   15.___
    make every effort to help youthful delinquents to solve
    their problems while they are living in the community.
    However, when a youth is consistently in trouble and is
    self-destructive, the BEST course of action would be for
    the worker to
    A. try to stay with him as much as possible to provide
       supervision and keep him out of trouble
    B. report him to the principal of his school
    ✓C. support his being sent to a training school or other
       institution
    D. urge him to join a school athletic team, so that the
       coach can keep an eye on him

16. Because street youth groups vary widely in their makeup   16.___
    and patterns of behavior, it is important for the worker
    to
    A. work only with those groups that are prepared to
       come into a youth center and abide by its rules
    B. develop a single approach that can be applied to
       all gangs
    C. concentrate only on groups that are likely to
       benefit from help
    ✓D. use varied approaches in order to suit the patterns
       of different groups and problem individuals

17. Voluntary social agencies based in disadvantaged neigh-   17.___
    borhoods often fail to meet the needs of the poor people
    living in the community.
    Of the following, the MOST likely reason for such failure
    is
    ✓A. lack of participation by the local poor in planning
       the programs of the agency
    B. inefficient administration of the agency
    C. inability of the local poor to contribute funds to
       the agency
    D. lack of interest on the part of the poor because of
       increased availability of public funds for local
       projects

18. A worker learns that the settlement house in his assigned   18.___
    area, which has a contract with the youth services agency
    and has agreed to provide services for all neighborhood
    youths, refuses to allow members of his group to use the
    center's facilities.

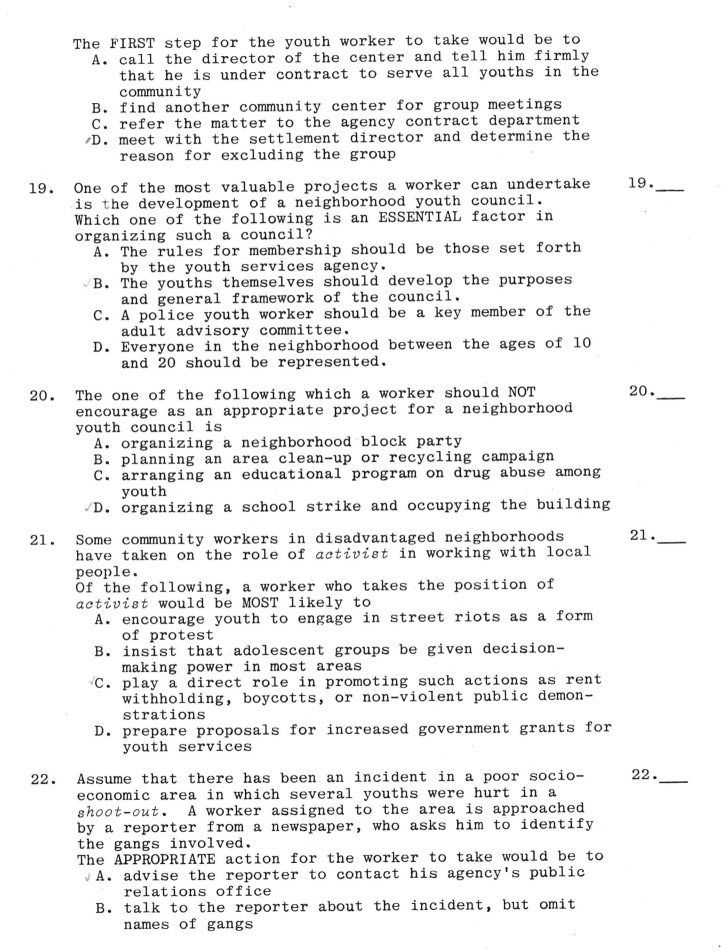

The FIRST step for the youth worker to take would be to
   A. call the director of the center and tell him firmly
      that he is under contract to serve all youths in the
      community
   B. find another community center for group meetings
   C. refer the matter to the agency contract department
  ✓D. meet with the settlement director and determine the
      reason for excluding the group

19. One of the most valuable projects a worker can undertake   19.___
    is the development of a neighborhood youth council.
    Which one of the following is an ESSENTIAL factor in
    organizing such a council?
      A. The rules for membership should be those set forth
         by the youth services agency.
     ✓B. The youths themselves should develop the purposes
         and general framework of the council.
      C. A police youth worker should be a key member of the
         adult advisory committee.
      D. Everyone in the neighborhood between the ages of 10
         and 20 should be represented.

20. The one of the following which a worker should NOT   20.___
    encourage as an appropriate project for a neighborhood
    youth council is
      A. organizing a neighborhood block party
      B. planning an area clean-up or recycling campaign
      C. arranging an educational program on drug abuse among
         youth
     ✓D. organizing a school strike and occupying the building

21. Some community workers in disadvantaged neighborhoods   21.___
    have taken on the role of *activist* in working with local
    people.
    Of the following, a worker who takes the position of
    activist would be MOST likely to
      A. encourage youth to engage in street riots as a form
         of protest
      B. insist that adolescent groups be given decision-
         making power in most areas
     ✓C. play a direct role in promoting such actions as rent
         withholding, boycotts, or non-violent public demon-
         strations
      D. prepare proposals for increased government grants for
         youth services

22. Assume that there has been an incident in a poor socio-   22.___
    economic area in which several youths were hurt in a
    shoot-out. A worker assigned to the area is approached
    by a reporter from a newspaper, who asks him to identify
    the gangs involved.
    The APPROPRIATE action for the worker to take would be to
     ✓A. advise the reporter to contact his agency's public
         relations office
      B. talk to the reporter about the incident, but omit
         names of gangs

C. give the reporter any facts he has
D. tell the reporter that, in order to be able to work
with gangs, he cannot become involved with the press

23. Assume that a worker who is planning to escort a 17-year-   23.___
old youth in his group to court is asked to testify in
the youth's behalf by the youth's attorney.
The MOST advisable course of action for the worker to
take would be to
A. testify in order to help the youth
B. consult his supervisor in order to arrive at a decision about testifying
C. refuse to testify
D. refuse to testify unless he can get permission from
the youth's parents

24. A worker is approached by some members of a group called   24.___
Latin Lads, who tell him that they are now a social club
and would like him to help them incorporate the club in
order to get a charter.
The worker should FIRST
A. tell the group that this is not his job function
B. contact a lawyer to help the group
C. attempt to convince members to get responsible
adults in the community involved in helping them get
a charter
D. discuss the process of getting a charter with the
group and offer his name as a responsible adult

25. The community assistance function of a youth services   25.___
agency is CORRECTLY described as follows:
A. Screening applications of community groups for federal
grants to run summer youth programs
B. Providing technical assistance to existing youth-
serving organizations and helping communities to
develop the additional resources needed to solve
the most critical youth problems
C. Mediating problems of jurisdiction among public and
private community organizations serving youth
D. Improving liaison between the police, the courts, and
public and private community organizations serving
youth, regarding juvenile offenders

KEY (CORRECT ANSWERS)

1. A	6. B	11. A	16. D	21. C
2. A	7. B	12. A	17. A	22. A
3. A	8. C	13. B	18. D	23. B
4. C	9. A	14. D	19. B	24. C
5. B	10. C	15. C	20. D	25. B

TEST 2

Questions 1-5.

DIRECTIONS: Questions 1 through 5 are to be answered SOLELY on the basis of the following paragraph.

There are several different schools of thought about the causes of juvenile delinquency. According to the "cultural-transmission" school of thought, delinquency is neither inborn nor developed independently. Children learn to become delinquents as members of groups in which delinquent conduct is already established and "the thing to do." This school maintains that a child need not be different from other children or have any problems or defects of personality or intelligence in order to become a delinquent. On the other hand, the "psychogenic" school views delinquency as a method of coping with some underlying problem of adjustment. This school also holds that the tendency to become delinquent is not inherited. The delinquent, however, has frustrations, deprivations, insecurities, anxieties, guilt feelings or mental conflicts which differ in kind or degree from those of non-delinquent children. Delinquency is thought of as a symptom of the underlying problem of adjustment in the same way as a fever is a symptom of an underlying infection. According to this school, if other children exhibit the same behavior, it is because they have independently found a similar solution to their problems.

1. Of the following, the MOST suitable title for the fore-   1.___
   going paragraph would be
   - A. Problems in the Scientific Study of Juvenile Delin-
     quency
   - B. The Effect of Disturbed Family Situations
   - C. Two Theories of Juvenile Delinquency
   - D. Solutions to a Major Social Problem

2. According to the paragraph, the *cultural-transmission*   2.___
   school of thought holds that there is a definite relationship between juvenile delinquency and the youths'
   - A. intelligence   B. psychological problems
   - C. family problems   D. choice of friends

3. According to the paragraph, of the following, both schools   3.___
   of thought reject as a cause of juvenile delinquency the
   factor of
   - A. guilt feelings   B. inherited traits
   - C. repeated frustration   D. extreme insecurities

4. On the basis of the paragraph, which of the following
   statements is CORRECT?   4.___
   The
   A. *cultural-transmission* school of thought maintains
      that a child independently develops delinquent
      behavior as a solution to his problems
   B. *psychogenic* school of thought holds that children
      become delinquents because it is
   C. *cultural-transmission* school of thought maintains
      that delinquency is the visible symptom of an under-
      lying personality problem
   D. *psychogenic* school of thought holds that delinquents
      have mental conflicts that differ in kind or degree
      from non-delinquents

5. The author's attitude toward these schools of thought is   5.___
   that he
   A. describes them objectively without indicating par-
      tiality to either school of thought
   B. favors the *cultural-transmission* school of thought
   C. favors the *psychogenic* school of thought
   D. suggests that he thinks both schools of thought are
      incorrect

Questions 6-10.

DIRECTIONS: Questions 6 through 10 are to be answered SOLELY on the
            basis of the following paragraph.

*When a young boy or girl is released from one of the various
facilities operated by the Division for Youth, supportive services
to help the youth face community, group, and family pressures are
needed as much as, if not more than, at any other time. These
services are the responsibility of two units of the Division for
Youth, the Aftercare Unit, which serves youths discharged from the
urban homes, camps, and START Centers, and the Community Service
Bureaus, which serve youths released from the division's school and
center programs. To assure that supportive services for released
youths are easily identifiable and accessible, the division has
developed the "store-front" services center, located in the heart of
those areas to which many of the youngsters are returning. The
storefront concept and structure is able to coordinate more closely
services to the particular needs and situation of the youths and to
draw on the feeling of community participation and achievement by
persuading the community to join in helping them.*

6. Of the following, the BEST description of the storefront   6.___
   services center's relationship to neighborhood residents
   is that it
   A. actively encourages their participation
   B. accepts their help when offered
   C. asks neighborhood residents to develop rehabilitation
      programs
   D. limits participation to qualified neighborhood
      professional youth workers

7. On the basis of the paragraph, which of the following statements is CORRECT? 7.___
   A. Supportive services are not needed as much after a youth is released from a facility as during his stay.
   B. Storefront services centers are located near the facilities operated by the Division for Youth.
   C. The Community Service Bureaus serve youths released from urban homes.
   D. Youths are given supportive services in their communities after release from facilities operated by the Division for Youth.

8. Of the following, the MOST suitable title for the foregoing paragraph would be 8.___
   A. Problems of Youths Returning to Society
   B. Community, Group, and Family Pressures on Released Youths
   C. Neighborhood Supportive Services for Released Youths
   D. A Survey of Facilities Operated by the Division for Youth

9. Which of the following characteristics of the storefront services is mentioned in the paragraph? 9.___
   A. Cost   B. Availability
   C. Size   D. Complexity

10. On the basis of the paragraph, which of the following statements about the Aftercare Unit is INCORRECT? 10.___
    It
    A. is a part of the Division for Youth
    B. serves youths released from school programs
    C. is similar in function to the Community Service Bureaus
    D. was partly responsible for the development of storefront centers

Questions 11-20.

DIRECTIONS: In Questions 11 through 20, choose the lettered word or expression which is closest to the meaning of the first word or expression, *as used most frequently by street-oriented youth and members of youth gangs.* Do not try to give the usually accepted or dictionary definition of the word or expression.

11. copping 11.___
    A. stealing   B. lying
    C. squealing   D. harassing policemen

12. a geese 12.___
    A. stool pigeon   B. pulling a robbery
    C. lady pusher   D. free trip

13. jive stud   13.___
    A. lying braggart   B. wealthy drug pusher
    C. youth on probation   D. male prostitute with soul

14. turkey   14.___
    A. person easily manipulated by a gang member
    B. person who has been mugged
    C. discarded weapon
    D. beat-up car

15. a Jones   15.___
    A. a need for a fix   B. an alias
    C. a drug pusher   D. a fight for status

16. copping a plea   16.___
    A. testifying in court
    B. making up an excuse
    C. admitting guilt as originally charged
    D. asking a policeman for a favor

17. cold turkey   17.___
    A. giving up drugs
    B. kicking drugs without medication
    C. concealing a body
    D. keeping cool

18. dolls   18.___
    A. homosexuals   B. policewomen
    C. LSD   D. amphetamines

19. fair one   19.___
    A. heroin of good quality
    B. likeable white man
    C. fight between individual gang members
    D. rumble between two equal gangs

20. piece   20.___
    A. portion   B. loot   C. gun   D. pot

21. A good resource for a youth or adult who wants help in   21.___
finding employment or obtaining job training is the
    A. neighborhood manpower service center
    B. equal employment opportunity commission
    C. federation employment and guidance service
    D. economic development administration

22. It would be APPROPRIATE for a worker to refer a youth   22.___
who is interested in vocational training in such fields
as keypunch operation, business machine repair, or food
services to the organization called
    A. Opportunities Industrialization Center
    B. Job Corps
    C. DSW Training Institute
    D. College for Human Services

23. Which of the following is a large group of business, religious, and educational institutions, labor unions, and community organizations which have united in order to find solutions to the problems of poverty and urban decay?
    A. New York Urban Coalition, Inc.
    B. Massive Neighborhood Economic Development, Inc.
    C. Council Against Poverty
    D. Interfaith Citywide Coordinating Committee Against Poverty

23.___

24. Which one of the following institutions for the care of adolescent boys is under the Department of Social Services?
    A. Jennings Hall
    B. New Hampton School for Boys
    C. Lincoln Hall
    D. Stuyvesant Residence Club

24.___

25. The Metropolitan Applied Research Center, Inc., which is headed by Kenneth B. Clark, is CORRECTLY described as a

25.___
    A. national organization which aims to improve living conditions of lower-income urban residents through research, analysis, strategy development, and intervention in areas such as economic opportunity, education, housing, health and welfare services, and consumer protection
    B. city agency which provides individual and group psychotherapy for patients of all ages, races, and creeds and information and education in healthy emotional living through interaction with all segments of the community
    C. branch of Metropolitan Hospital which includes guidance services for children and adolescents and drug addiction, mental hygiene, and psychiatric walk-in clinics
    D. central city organization which fosters joint planning and participation of governmental and voluntary social welfare organizations in research in the field of human services

KEY (CORRECT ANSWERS)

1. C	6. A	11. A	16. B	21. A
2. D	7. D	12. B	17. B	22. A
3. B	8. C	13. A	18. D	23. A
4. D	9. B	14. A	19. C	24. A
5. A	10. B	15. A	20. C	25. A

EXAMINATION SECTION
TEST 1

1. In public agencies, communications should be based PRIMARILY on a
    A. two-way flow from the top down and from the bottom up, most of which should be given in writing to avoid ambiguity
    B. multidirection flow among all levels and with outside persons
    C. rapid, internal one-way flow from the top down
    D. two-way flow of information, most of which should be given orally for purposes of clarity

1.___

2. In some organizations, changes in policy or procedures are often communicated by word of mouth from supervisors to employees with no prior discussion or exchange of view-points with employees.
This procedure often produces employee dissatisfaction CHIEFLY because
    A. information is mostly unusable since a considerable amount of time is required to transmit information
    B. lower-level supervisors tend to be excessively concerned with minor details
    C. management has failed to seek employees' advice before making changes
    D. valuable staff time is lost between decision-making and the implementation of decisions

2.___

3. For good letter writing, you should try to visualize the person to whom you are writing, especially if you know him.
Of the following rules, it is LEAST helpful in such visualization to think of
    A. the person's likes and dislikes, his concerns, and his needs
    B. what you would be likely to say if speaking in person
    C. what you would expect to be asked if speaking in person
    ✓D. your official position in order to be certain that your words are proper

3.___

4. One approach to good informal letter writing is to make letters sound conversational.
All of the following practices will usually help to do this EXCEPT:
    A. If possible, use a style which is similar to the style used when speaking

4.___

√B. Substitute phrases for single words (e.g., *at the present time* for *now*
C. Use contractions of words (e.g., *you're* for *you are*)
D. Use ordinary vocabulary when possible

5. All of the following rules will aid in producing clarity in report-writing EXCEPT:
   A. Give specific details or examples, if possible
   B. Keep related words close together in each sentence
   C. Present information in sequential order
   √D. Put several thoughts or ideas in each paragraph

6. The one of the following statements about public relations which is MOST accurate is that
   A. in the long run, appearance gains better results than performance
   B. objectivity is decreased if outside public relations consultants are employed
   √C. public relations is the responsibility of every employee
   D. public relations should be based on a formal publicity program

7. The form of communication which is usually considered to be MOST personally directed to the intended recipient is the
   A. brochure   B. film   √C. letter   D. radio

8. In general, a document that presents an organization's views or opinions on a particular topic is MOST accurately known as a
   A. tear sheet   √B. position paper
   C. flyer   D. journal

9. Assume that you have been asked to speak before an organization of persons who oppose a newly announced program in which you are involved. You feel tense about talking to this group.
   Which of the following rules generally would be MOST useful in gaining rapport when speaking before the audience?
   A. Impress them with your experience
   B. Stress all areas of disagreement
   √C. Talk to the group as to one person
   D. Use formal grammar and language

10. An organization must have an effective public relations program since, at its best, public relations is a bridge to change.
    All of the following statements about communication and human behavior have validity EXCEPT:
    A. People are more likely to talk about controversial matters with like-minded people than with those holding other views

B. The earlier an experience, the more powerful its effect since it influences how later experiences will be interpreted

√C. In periods of social tension, official sources gain increased believability

D. Those who are already interested in a topic are the ones who are most open to receive new communications about it

11. An employee should be encouraged to talk easily and frankly when he is dealing with his supervisor. In order to encourage such free communication, it would be MOST appropriate for a supervisor to behave in a(n)
   √A. sincere manner; assure the employee that you will deal with him honestly and openly
   B. official manner; you are a supervisor and must always act formally with subordinates
   C. investigative manner; you must probe and question to get to a basis of trust
   D. unemotional manner; the employee's emotions and background should play no part in your dealings with him

11.___

12. Research findings show that an increase in free communication within an agency GENERALLY results in which one of the following?
   √A. Improved morale and productivity
   B. Increased promotional opportunities
   C. An increase in authority
   D. A spirit of honesty

12.___

13. Assume that you are a supervisor and your superiors have given you a new-type procedure to be followed. Before passing this information on to your subordinates, the one of the following actions that you should take FIRST is to
   A. ask your superiors to send out a memorandum to the entire staff
   √B. clarify the procedure in your own mind
   C. set up a training course to provide instruction on the new procedure
   D. write a memorandum to your subordinates

13.___

14. Communication is necessary for an organization to be effective. The one of the following which is LEAST important for most communication systems is that
   A. messages are sent quickly and directly to the person who needs them to operate
   B. information should be conveyed understandably and accurately
   √C. the method used to transmit information should be kept secret so that security can be maintained
   D. senders of messages must know how their messages are received and acted upon

14.___

15. Which one of the following is the CHIEF advantage of   15.__
    listening willingly to subordinates and encouraging them
    to talk freely and honestly?
    It
    ✓A. reveals to supervisors the degree to which ideas that
        are passed down are accepted by subordinates
    B. reduces the participation of subordinates in the
       operation of the department
    C. encourages subordinates to try for promotion
    D. enables supervisors to learn more readily what the
       grapevine is saying

16. A supervisor may be informed through either oral or written 16.__
    reports.
    Which one of the following is an ADVANTAGE of using oral
    reports?
    A. There is no need for a formal record of the report.
    B. An exact duplicate of the report is not easily
       transmitted to others.
    C. A good oral report requires little time for prepara-
       tion.
    ✓D. An oral report involves two-way communication between
        a subordinate and his supervisor.

17. Of the following, the MOST important reason why supervisors 17.__
    should communicate effectively with the public is to
    A. improve the public's understanding of information
       that is important for them to know
    B. establish a friendly relationship
    C. obtain information about the kinds of people who
       come to the agency
    D. convince the public that services are adequate

18. Supervisors should generally NOT use phrases like *too*   18.__
    hard, *too easy*, and *a lot* PRINCIPALLY because such phrases
    A. may be offensive to some minority groups
    B. are too informal
    ✓C. mean different things to different people
    D. are difficult to remember

19. The ability to communicate clearly and concisely is an   19.__
    important element in effective leadership.
    Which of the following statements about oral and written
    communication is GENERALLY true?
    A. Oral communication is more time-consuming.
    ✓B. Written communication is more likely to be misinter-
        preted.
    C. Oral communication is useful only in emergencies.
    D. Written communication is useful mainly when giving
       information to fewer than twenty people.

20. Rumors can often have harmful and disruptive effects on   20.___
an organization.
Which one of the following is the BEST way to prevent
rumors from becoming a problem?
    A. Refuse to act on rumors, thereby making them less
       believable.
    B. Increase the amount of information passed along by
       the *grapevine*.
    C. Distribute as much factual information as possible.
    D. Provide training in report writing.

21. Suppose that a subordinate asks you about a rumor he has   21.___
heard. The rumor deals with a subject which your superiors
consider *confidential*.
Which of the following BEST describes how you should
answer the subordinate?
Tell
    A. the subordinate that you don't make the rules and
       that he should speak to higher ranking officials
    B. the subordinate that you will ask your superior for
       information
    C. him only that you cannot comment on the matter
    D. him the rumor is not true

22. Supervisors often find it difficult to *get their message*   22.___
across when instructing newly appointed employees in their
various duties.
The MAIN reason for this is generally that the
    A. duties of the employees have increased
    B. supervisor is often so expert in his area that he
       fails to see it from the learner's point of view
    C. supervisor adapts his instruction to the slowest
       learner in the group
    D. new employees are younger, less concerned with job
       security and more interested in fringe benefits

23. Assume that you are discussing a job problem with an   23.___
employee under your supervision. During the discussion,
you see that the man's eyes are turning away from you
and that he is not paying attention.
In order to get the man's attention, you should FIRST
    A. ask him to look you in the eye
    B. talk to him about sports
    C. tell him he is being very rude
    D. change your tone of voice

24. As a supervisor, you may find it necessary to conduct   24.___
meetings with your subordinates.
Of the following, which would be MOST helpful in assuring
that a meeting accomplishes the purpose for which it was
called?
    A. Give notice of the conclusions you would like to
       reach at the start of the meeting.
    B. Delay the start of the meeting until everyone is
       present.

C. Write down points to be discussed in proper sequence.
D. Make sure everyone is clear on whatever conclusions have been reached and on what must be done after the meeting.

25. Every supervisor will occasionally be called upon to deliver a reprimand to a subordinate. If done properly, this can greatly help an employee improve his performance. Which one of the following is NOT a good practice to follow when giving a reprimand?
    A. Maintain your composure and temper.
    B. Reprimand a subordinate in the presence of other employees so they can learn the same lesson.
    C. Try to understand why the employee was not able to perform satisfactorily.
    D. Let your knowledge of the man involved determine the exact nature of the reprimand.

25.

————

1. C		11. A	
2. B		12. A	
3. D		13. B	
4. B		14. C	
5. D		15. A	
6. C		16. D	
7. C		17. A	
8. B		18. C	
9. C		19. B	
10. C		20. C	

21. B
22. B
23. D
24. D
25. B

————

TEST 2

DIRECTIONS: Each question or incomplete statement is followed by
                several suggested answers or completions. Select the
                one that BEST answers the question or completes the
                statement. *PRINT THE LETTER OF THE CORRECT ANSWER IN
                THE SPACE AT THE RIGHT.*

1. Usually one thinks of communication as a single step,   1.___
    essentially that of transmitting an idea.
    Actually, however, this is only part of a total process,
    the FIRST step of which should be
        A. the prompt dissemination of the idea to those who may
           be affected by it
        B. motivating those affected to take the required action
        C. clarifying the idea in one's own mind
        D. deciding to whom the idea is to be communicated

2. Research studies on patterns of informal communication   2.___
    have concluded that most individuals in a group tend to be
    passive recipients of news, while a few make it their
    business to spread it around in an organization.
    With this conclusion in mind, it would be MOST correct for
    the supervisor to attempt to identify these few individuals
    and
        A. give them the complete facts on important matters in
           advance of others
        B. inform the other subordinates of the identify of these
           few individuals so that their influence may be
           minimized
        C. keep them straight on the facts on important matters
        D. warn them to cease passing along any information to
           others

3. The one of the following which is the PRINCIPAL advantage   3.___
    of making an oral report is that it
        A. affords an immediate opportunity for two-way communi-
           cation between the subordinate and superior
        B. is an easy method for the superior to use in trans-
           mitting information to others of equal rank
        C. saves the time of all concerned
        D. permits more precise pinpointing of praise or blame
           by means of follow-up questions by the superior

4. An agency may sometimes undertake a public relations   4.___
    program of a defensive nature.
    With reference to the use of defensive public relations,
    it would be MOST correct to state that it
        A. is bound to be ineffective since defensive statements,
           even though supported by factual data, can never hope
           to even partly overcome the effects of prior unfavor-
           able attacks

B. proves that the agency has failed to establish good
relationships with newspapers, radio stations, or
other means of publicity
C. shows that the upper echelons of the agency have
failed to develop sound public relations procedures
and techniques
✓D. is sometimes required to aid morale by protecting
the agency from unjustified criticism and misunder-
standing of policies or procedures

5. Of the following factors which contribute to possible
undesirable public attitudes towards an agency, the one
which is MOST susceptible to being changed by the efforts
of the individual employee in an organization is that
A. enforcement of unpopular regulations has offended
many individuals
B. the organization itself has an unsatisfactory reputation
C. the public is not interested in agency matters
✓D. there are many errors in judgment committed by
individual subordinates

6. It is not enough for an agency's services to be of a high
quality; attention must also be given to the acceptability
of these services to the general public.
This statement is GENERALLY
A. *false*; a superior quality of service automatically
wins public support
✓B. *true*; the agency cannot generally progress beyond the
understanding and support of the public
C. *false*; the acceptance by the public of agency services
determines their quality
D. *true*; the agency is generally unable to engage in any
effective enforcement activity without public support

7. Sustained agency participation in a program sponsored by
a community organization is MOST justified when
✓A. the achievement of agency objectives in some area
depends partly on the activity of this organization
B. the community organization is attempting to widen the
base of participation in all community affairs
C. the agency is uncertain as to what the community wants
D. there is an obvious lack of good leadership in a
newly formed community organization

8. Of the following, the LEAST likely way in which a records
system may serve a supervisor is in
A. developing a sympathetic and cooperative public
attitude toward the agency
B. improving the quality of supervision by permitting a
check on the accomplishment of subordinates
✓C. permit a precise prediction of the exact incidences
in specific categories for the following year
D. helping to take the guesswork out of the distribution
of the agency

5.__
6.__
7.__
8.__

9. Assuming that the *grapevine* in any organization is
   virtually indestructible, the one of the following which
   it is MOST important for management to understand is:
     A. What is being spread by means of the *grapevine* and
       the reason for spreading it
     B. What is being spread by means of the *grapevine* and
       how it is being spread
     C. Who is involved in spreading the information that is
       on the *grapevine*
     D. Why those who are involved in spreading the informa-
       tion are doing so

9.___

10. When the supervisor writes a report concerning an investi-
    gation to which he has been assigned, it should be LEAST
    intended to provide
      A. a permanent official record of relevant information
        gathered
      B. a summary of case findings limited to facts which tend
        to indicate the guilt of a suspect
      C. a statement of the facts on which higher authorities
        may base a corrective or disciplinary action
      D. other investigators with information so that they may
        continue with other phases of the investigation

10.___

11. In survey work, questionnaires rather than interviews are
    sometimes used.
    The one of the following which is a DISADVANTAGE of the
    questionnaire method as compared with the interview is the
      A. difficulty of accurately interpreting the results
      B. problem of maintaining anonymity of the participant
      C. fact that it is relatively uneconomical
      D. requirement of special training for the distribution
        of questionnaires

11.___

12. In his contacts with the public, an employee should
    attempt to create a good climate of support for his agency.
    This statement is GENERALLY
      A. *false*; such attempts are clearly beyond the scope of
        his responsibility
      B. *true*; employees of an agency who come in contact with
        the public have the opportunity to affect public
        relations
      C. *false*; such activity should be restricted to super-
        visors trained in public relations techniques
      D. *true*; the future expansion of the agency depends to
        a great extent on continued public support of the
        agency

12.___

13. The repeated use by a supervisor of a call for volunteers
    to get a job done is objectionable MAINLY because it
      A. may create a feeling of animosity between the
        volunteers and the non-volunteers
      B. may indicate that the supervisor is avoiding respon-
        sibility for making assignments which will be most
        productive

13.___

   C. is an indication that the supervisor is not familiar
      with the individual capabilities of his men
   D. is unfair to men who, for valid reasons, do not, or
      cannot volunteer

14. Of the following statements concerning subordinates'
    expressions to a supervisor of their opinions and feelings
    concerning work situations, the one which is MOST correct
    is that
    A. by listening and responding to such expressions the
       supervisor encourages the development of complaints
    B. the lack of such expressions should indicate to the
       supervisor that there is a high level of job
       satisfaction
    C. the more the supervisor listens to and responds to
       such expressions, the more he demonstrates lack of
       supervisory ability
  √ D. by listening and responding to such expressions, the
       supervisor will enable many subordinates to under-
       stand and solve their own problems on the job

15. In attempting to motivate employees, rewards are con-
    sidered preferable to punishment PRIMARILY because
    A. punishment seldom has any effect on human behavior
    B. punishment usually results in decreased production
    C. supervisors find it difficult to punish
  √ D. rewards are more likely to result in willing coopera-
       tion

16. In an attempt to combat the low morale in his organization,
    a high-level supervisor publicized an *open-door* policy to
    allow employees who wished to do so to come to him with
    their complaints.
    Which of the following is LEAST likely to account for the
    fact that no employee came in with a complaint?
    A. Employees are generally reluctant to go over the
       heads of their immediate supervisors.
    B. The employees did not feel that management would
       help them.
  √ C. The low morale was not due to complaints associated
       with the job.
    D. The employees felt that they had more to lose than
       to gain.

17. It is MOST desirable to use written instructions rather
    than oral instructions for a particular job when
    A. a mistake on the job will not be serious
    B. the job can be completed in a short time
    C. there is no need to explain the job minutely
  √ D. the job involves many details

18. If you receive a telephone call regarding a matter which
    your office does not handle, you should FIRST   18.___
    A. give the caller the telephone number of the proper
       office so that he can dial again
    ✓B. offer to transfer the caller to the proper office
    C. suggest that the caller re-dial since he probably
       dialed incorrectly
    D. tell the caller he has reached the wrong office and
       then hang up

19. When you answer the telephone, the MOST important reason   19.___
    for identifying yourself and your organization is to
    A. give the caller time to collect his or her thoughts
    B. impress the caller with your courtesy
    ✓C. inform the caller that he or she has reached the
       right number
    D. set a business-like tone at the beginning of the
       conversation

20. As soon as you pick up the phone, a very angry caller   20.___
    begins immediately to complain about city agencies and
    red tape. He says that he has been shifted to two or
    three different offices. It turns out that he is seeking
    information which is not immediately available to you.
    You believe you know, however, where it can be found.
    Which of the following actions is the BEST one for you
    to take?
    A. To eliminate all confusion, suggest that the caller
       write the agency stating explicitly what he wants.
    B. Apologize by telling the caller how busy city
       agencies now are, but also tell him directly that
       you do not have the information he needs.
    ✓C. Ask for the caller's telephone number and assure
       him you will call back after you have checked further.
    D. Give the caller the name and telephone number of the
       person who might be able to help, but explain that
       you are not positive he will get results.

21. Which of the following approaches usually provides the   21.___
    BEST communication in the objectives and values of a
    new program which is to be introduced?
    A. A general written description of the program by the
       program manager for review by those who share
       responsibility
    B. An effective verbal presentation by the program
       manager to those affected
    ✓C. Development of the plan and operational approach in
       carrying out the program by the program manager
       assisted by his key subordinates
    D. Development of the plan by the program manager's
       supervisor

22. What is the BEST approach for introducing change?

22._

A

  ✓A. combination of written and also verbal communication to all personnel affected by the change
  B. general bulletin to all personnel
  C. meeting pointing out all the values of the new approach
  D. written directive to key personnel

23. Of the following, committees are BEST used for

23._

  ✓A. advising the head of the organization
  B. improving functional work
  C. making executive decisions
  D. making specific planning decisions

24. An effective discussion leader is one who

24._

  A. announces the problem and his preconceived solution at the start of the discussion
  ✓B. guides and directs the discussion according to pre-arranged outline
  C. interrupts or corrects confused participants to save time
  D. permits anyone to say anything at anytime

25. The human relations movement in management theory is BASICALLY concerned with

25._

  A. counteracting employee unrest
  B. eliminating the *time and motion* man
  ✓C. interrelationships among individuals in organizations
  D. the psychology of the worker

KEY (CORRECT ANSWERS)

1. C		11. A	
2. C		12. B	
3. A		13. B	
4. D		14. D	
5. D		15. D	
6. B		16. C	
7. A		17. D	
8. C		18. B	
9. A		19. C	
10. B		20. C	

21. C
22. A
23. A
24. B
25. C

EXAMINATION SECTION

TEST 1

DIRECTIONS: Each question or incomplete statement is followed by several suggested answers or completions. Select the one that BEST answers the question or completes the statement. *PRINT THE LETTER OF THE CORRECT ANSWER IN THE SPACE AT THE RIGHT.*

1. One of the responsibilities of the supervisor is to provide top administration with information about clients and their problems that will help in the evaluation of existing policies and indicate the need for modifications. In order to fulfill this responsibility, it would be MOST essential for the supervisor to
    A. routinely forward all regularly prepared and recurrent reports from his subordinates to his immediate superior
    B. regularly review agency rules, regulations, and policies to make sure that he has sufficient knowledge to make appropriate analyses
    C. note repeated instances of failure of staff to correctly administer a policy and schedule staff conferences for corrective training
    D. analyze reports on cases submitted by subordinates in order to select relevant trend material to be forwarded to his superiors

1.____

2. You find that your division has a serious problem because of unusually long delays in filing reports and overdue approvals to private agencies under contract for services. The MOST appropriate step to take FIRST in this situation would be to
    A. request additional staff to work on reports and approvals
    B. order staff to work overtime until the backlog is eliminated
    C. impress staff with the importance of expeditious handling of reports and approvals
    D. analyze present procedures for handling reports and approvals

2.____

3. When a supervisor finds that he must communicate orally information that is significant enough to affect the entire staff, it would be MOST important to
    A. distribute a written summary of the information to his staff before discussing it orally
    B. tell his subordinate supervisors to discuss this information at individual conferences with their subordinates
    C. call a follow-up meeting of absentees as soon as they return
    D. restate and summarize the information in order to make sure that everyone understands its meaning and implications

3.____

4. Of the following, the BEST way for a supervisor to assist   4.___
   a subordinate who has unusually heavy work pressures is to
      A. point out that such pressures go with the job and
         must be tolerated
      B. suggest to him that the pressures probably result
         from poor handling of his workload
     ✓C. help him to be selective in deciding on priorities
         during the period of pressure
      D. ask him to work overtime until the period of pressure
         is over

5. Leadership is a basic responsibility of the supervisor.   5.___
   The one of the following which would be the LEAST appropriate way to fulfill this role is for the supervisor to
      A. help staff to work up to their capacities in every
         possible way
      B. encourage independent judgment and actions by staff
         members
      C. allow staff to participate in decisions within policy
         limits
     ✓D. take over certain tasks in which he is more competent
         than his subordinates

6. Assume that you have assigned a very difficult administra-   6.___
   tive task to one of your best subordinate supervisors, but
   he is reluctant to take it on because he fears that he will
   fail in it. It is your judgment, however, that he is quite
   capable of performing this task.
   The one of the following which is the MOST desirous way
   for you to handle this situation is to
     ✓A. reassure him that he has enough skill to perform the
         task and that he will not be penalized if he fails
      B. reassign the task to another supervisor who is more
         achievement-oriented and more confident of his skills
      C. minimize the importance of the task so that he will
         feel it is safe for him to attempt it
      D. stress the importance of the task and the dependence
         of the other staff members on his succeeding in it

7. Assume that a member of your professional staff deliberate-   7.___
   ly misinterprets a new state directive because he fears
   that its enforcement will have an adverse effect on clients.
   Although you consider him to be a good supervisor and
   basically agree with him, you should direct him to comply.
   Of the following, the MOST desirable way for you to handle
   this situation would be to
      A. avoid a confrontation with him by transferring respon-
         sibility for carrying out the directive to another
         member of your staff
      B. explain to him that you are in a better position than
         he to assess the implications of the new directive
     ✓C. discuss with him the basic reasons for his misinter-
         pretation and explain why he must comply with the
         directive
      D. allow him to interpret the directive in his own way
         as long as he assumes full responsibility for his
         actions

8. Of the following, the MAIN reason it is important for an   8.___
administrator in a large organization to properly coordinate the work delegated to subordinates is that such
coordination
   A. makes it unnecessary to hold frequent staff meetings
and conferences with key staff members
   B. reduces the necessity for regular evaluation of
procedures and programs, production, and performance
of personnel
   C. results in greater economy and stricter accountability for the organization's resources
   D. facilitates integration of the contributions of the
numerous staff members who are responsible for specific parts of the total workload

9. The one of the following which would NOT be an appropriate   9.___
reason for the formulation of an entirely new policy is
that it would
   A. serve as a positive affirmation of the agency's function and how it is to be carried out
   B. give focus and direction to the work of the staff,
particularly in decision-making
   C. inform the public of the precise conditions under
which services will be rendered
   D. provide procedures which constitute uniform methods
of carrying out operations

10. Of the following, it is MOST difficult to formulate   10.___
policy in an organization where
   A. work assignments are narrowly specialized by units
   B. staff members have varied backgrounds and a wide
range of competency
   C. units implementing the same policy are in the same
geographic location
   D. staff is experienced and fully trained

11. For a supervisor to feel that he is responsible for influ-   11.___
encing the attitudes of his staff members is GENERALLY
considered
   A. *undesirable*; attitudes of adults are emotional factors
which usually cannot be changed
   B. *desirable*; certain attitudes can be obstructive and
should be modified in order to provide effective
service to clients
   C. *undesirable*; the supervisor should be nonjudgmental
and accepting of widely different attitudes and
social patterns of staff members
   D. *desirable*; influencing attitudes is a teaching
responsibility which the supervisor shares with the
training specialist

12. The one of the following which is NOT generally a function   12.___
    of the higher-level supervisor is
    √A. projecting the budget and obtaining financial resources
     B. providing conditions conducive to optimum employee
        production
     C. maintaining records and reports as a basis for accoun-
        tability and evaluation
     D. evaluating program achievements and personnel effec-
        tiveness in accordance with goals and standards

13. As a supervisor in a recently decentralized services   13.___
    center offering multiple services, you are given respon-
    sibility for an orientation program for professional
    staff on the recent reorganization of the department.
    Of the following, the MOST appropriate step to take
    FIRST would be to
    √A. organize a series of workshops for subordinate super-
        visors
     B. arrange a tour of the new geographic area of service
     C. review supervisors' reports, statistical data, and
        other relevant material
     D. develop a resource manual for staff on the reorganized
        center

14. Experts generally agree that the content of training   14.___
    sessions should be closely related to workers' practice.
    Of the following, the BEST method of achieving this aim
    is for the training conference leader to
    √A. encourage group discussion of problems that concern
        staff in their practice
     B. develop closer working relationships with top
        administration
     C. coordinate with central office to obtain feedback on
        problems that concern staff
     D. observe workers in order to develop a pattern of
        problems for class discussion

15. The one of the following which is generally the MOST   15.___
    useful teaching tool for professional staff development is
     A. visual aids and tape recordings
     B. professional literature
    √C. agency case material
     D. lectures by experts

16. The one of the following which is NOT a good reason for   16.___
    using group conferences as a method of supervision is to
     A. give workers a feeling of mutual support through
        sharing common problems
    √B. save time by eliminating the need for individual
        conferences
     C. encourage discussion of certain problems that are
        not as likely to come up in individual conferences
     D. provide an opportunity for developing positive
        identification with the department and its programs

17. The supervisor, in his role as teacher, applies his
    teaching in line with his understanding of people and
    realizes that teaching is a highly individualized process,
    based on understanding of the worker as a person and as a
    learner.
    This statement implies MOST NEARLY that the supervisor
    must help the worker to
    A. overcome his biases
    B. develop his own ways of working
    C. gain confidence in his ability
    D. develop the will to work

17.___

18. Of the following, the circumstances under which it would
    be MOST appropriate to divide a training conference for
    professional staff into small workshops is when
    A. some of the trainees are not aware of the effect of
       their attitudes and behavior on others
    B. the trainees need to look at human relations problems
       from different perspectives
    C. the trainees are faced with several substantially
       different types of problems in their job assignments
    D. the trainees need to know how to function in many
       different capacities

18.___

19. Of the following, the MAIN reason why it is important to
    systematically evaluate a specific training program while
    it is in progress is to
    A. collect data that will serve as a valid basis for
       improving the agency's overall training program and
       maintaining control over its components
    B. insure that instruction by training specialists is
       conducted in a manner consistent with the planned
       design of the training program
    C. identify areas in which additional or remedial
       training for the training specialists can be planned
       and implemented
    D. provide data which are usable in effecting revisions
       of specific components of the training program

19.___

20. Staff development has been defined as an educational
    process which seeks to provide agency staff with knowledge
    about specific job responsibilities and to effect changes
    in staff attitudes and behavior patterns. Assume that
    you are assigned to define the educational objectives of
    a specific training program.
    In accordance with the above concept, the MOST helpful
    formulation would be a statement of the
    A. purpose and goals of each training session
    B. generalized patterns of behavior to be developed in
       the trainees
    C. content material to be presented in the training
       sessions
    D. kind of behavior to be developed in the trainees and
       the situations in which this behavior will be applied

20.___

21. In teaching personnel under your supervision how to gather and analyze facts before attempting to solve a problem, the one of the following training methods which would be MOST effective is

 ✓A. case study   B. role playing
  C. programmed learning   D. planned experience

                    21.____

22. Federal and state welfare agencies have been discussing the importance of analyzing functions traditionally included in the position of caseworker, with a view toward identifying and separating those activities to be performed by the most highly skilled personnel.
Of the following, an IMPORTANT secondary gain which can result from such differential use of staff is that

 ✓A. supporting job assignments can be given to persons unable to meet the demands of casework, to the satisfaction of all concerned
  B. documentation will be provided on workers who are not suited for all the duties now part of the caseworker's job
  C. caseworkers with a high level of competence in working with people can be rewarded through promotion or merit increases
  D. incompetent workers can be identified and categorized as a basis for transfer or separation from the service

                     22.____

23. Of the following, a serious DISADVANTAGE of a performance evaluation system based on standardized evaluation factors is that such a system tends to

  A. exacerbate the anxieties of those supervisors who are apprehensive about determining what happens to another person
  B. subject the supervisor to psychological stress by emphasizing the incompatibility of his dual role as both judge and counselor
  C. create organizational conflict by encouraging personnel who wish to enhance their standing to become too aggressive in the performance of their duties
 ✓D. lead many staff members to concentrate on measuring up in terms of the evaluation factors and to disregard other aspects of their work

                     23.____

24. Which of the following would contribute MOST to the achievement of conformity of staff activities and goals to the intent of agency policies and procedures?

 ✓A. Effective communications and organizational discipline
  B. Changing nature of the underlying principles and desired purpose of the policies and procedures
  C. Formulation of specific criteria for implementing the policies and procedures
  D. Continuous monitoring of the essential effectiveness of agency operations

                     24.____

25. Job enlargement, a management device used by large organi-   25.___
zations to counteract the adverse effects of specializa-
tion on employee performance, is LEAST likely to improve
employee motivation if it is accomplished by
   A. lengthening the job cycle and adding a large number
      of similar tasks
   B. allowing the employee to use a greater variety of
      skills
   C. increasing the scope and complexity of the employee's
      job
   D. giving the employee more opportunities to make
      decisions

KEY (CORRECT ANSWERS)

1. D	11. B
2. D	12. A
3. D	13. A
4. C	14. A
5. D	15. C
6. A	16. B
7. C	17. B
8. D	18. C
9. D	19. A
10. B	20. D

21. A
22. A
23. D
24. A
25. A

✓ TEST 2

1. When a supervisor requires approval for case action on a   1.___
    higher level, the process used is known as
    ✓A. administrative clearance
     B. going outside channels
     C. administrative consultation
     D. delegation of authority

2. In delegating authority to his subordinates, the one of   2.___
    the following to which a good supervisor should give
    PRIMARY consideration is the
    ✓A. results expected of them
     B. amount of power to be delegated
     C. amount of responsibility to be delegated
     D. their skill in the performance of present tasks

3. Of the following, the type of decision which could be   3.___
    SAFELY delegated to lower-level staff without undermining
    basic supervisory responsibility is one which
     A. involves a commitment that can be fulfilled only over
        a long period of time
     B. has fairly uncertain goals and promises
    ✓C. has the possibility of modification built into it
     D. may generate considerable resistance from those
        affected by it

4. Of the following, the MOST valuable contribution made by   4.___
    the informal organization in a large public service agency
    is that such an organization
     A. has goals and values which are usually consistent
        with and reinforce those of the formal organization
     B. is more flexible than the formal organization and
        more adaptable to changing conditions
     C. has a communications system which often contributes
        to the efficiency of the formal organization
     D. represents a sound basis on which to build the formal
        organizational structure

5. Of the following, the condition under which it would be   5.___
    MOST useful for a social services agency to develop
    detailed procedures is when
     A. subordinate supervisory personnel need a structure
        to help them develop greater independence
     B. employees have little experience or knowledge of how
        to perform certain assigned tasks

  C. coordination of agency activities is largely dependent upon personal contact
  D. agency activities must continually adjust to changes
   in local circumstances

6. Assume that a certain public agency administrator has the 6.___
  management philosophy that his agency's responsibility is
  to routinize existing operations, meet each day's problems
  as they arise, and resolve problems with a minimun of
  residual effect upon himself or his agency.
  The possibility that this official would be able to
  administer his agency without running into serious difficulties would be MORE likely during a period of
  A. economic change
  B. social change
  C. economic crisis
  D. social and economic stability

7. Some large organizations have adopted the practice of 7.___
  allowing each employee to establish his own performance
  goals, and then later evaluate himself in an individual
  conference with his immediate supervisor.
  Of the following, a DRAWBACK of this approach is that the
  employee
  A. may set his goals too low and rate himself too highly
  B. cannot control those variables which may improve his
   performance
  C. has no guidelines for improving his performance
  D. usually finds it more difficult to criticize himself
   than to accept criticism from others

8. Decentralization of services cannot completely eliminate 8.___
  the requirement of central office approval for certain
  case actions.
  The MOST valid reason for complaint about this requirement
  is that
  A. unavoidable delay created by referral to central office
   may cause serious problems for the client
  B. it may lower morals of supervisors who are not given
   the authority to take final action on urgent cases
  C. the concept of role responsibility is minimized
  D. the objective of delegated responsibility tends to
   be negated

9. Which of the following would be the MOST useful adminis- 9.___
  trative tool for the purpose of showing the sequence of
  operations and staff involved?
  A(n)
  A. organization chart
  B. flow chart
  C. manual of operating procedures
  D. statistical review

10. The prevailing pattern of organization in large public   10.___
    agencies consists of a limited span of control and organi-
    zation by function or, at lower levels, process.
    Of the following, the PRINCIPAL effect which this pattern
    or organization has on the management of work is that it
       A. reduces the management burden in significant ways
       B. creates a time lag between the perception of a problem
          and action on it
       C. makes it difficult to direct and observe employee
          performance
       D. facilitates the development of employees with mana-
          gerial ability

11. The one of the following which would be the MOST appropri-   11.___
    ate way to reduce tensions between line and staff personnel
    in public service agencies is to
       A. provide in-service training that will increase the
          sensitivity of line and staff personnel to their
          respective roles
       B. assign to staff personnel the role of providing
          assistance only when requested by line personnel
       C. separate staff from line personnel and provide staff
          with its own independent reward structure
       D. give line and staff personnel equal status in making
          decisions

12. In determining the appropriate span of control for sub-   12.___
    ordinate supervisors, which of the following principles
    should be followed?
    The more
       A. complex the work, the broader the effective span of
          control
       B. similar the jobs being supervised, the more narrow
          the effective span of control
       C. interdependent the jobs being supervised, the more
          narrow the effective span of control
       D. unpredictable the work, the broader the effective
          span of control

13. A method sometimes used in public service agencies to   13.___
    improve upward communication is to require subordinate
    supervisory staff to submit to top management monthly
    narrative reports of any problems which they deem
    important for consideration.
    Of the following, a MAJOR disadvantage of this method
    is that it may
       A. enable subordinate supervisors to avoid thinking
          about their problems by simply referring such matters
          to their superiors
       B. obscure important issues so that they are not given
          appropriate attention
       C. create a need for numerous staff conferences in order
          to handle all of the reported problems
       D. encourage some subordinate supervisors to focus on
          irrelevant matters and compete with each other in the
          length and content of their reports

14. The use of a committee as an approach to the problem of   14.___
    coordinating interdepartmental activities can present
    difficulties if the committee functions PRIMARILY as a(n)
       A. means of achieving personal objectives and goals
       B. instrument for coordinating activities that flow
          across departmental lines
       C. device for involving subordinate personnel in the
          decision-making process
       D. means of giving representation to competing interest
          groups

15. A study was recently made of the attitudes and perceptions 15.___
    of a sample of public assistance workers in nine New
    Jersey county welfare boards who had experienced a major
    organizational change and redefinition of their jobs as
    a result of separation of the income maintenance and
    social services functions. Questionnaires administered
    to these workers indicated that a disproportionate number
    of workers in the larger agencies were dissatisfied with
    the reorganization and their new assignments.
    Of the following, the MOST plausible reason for this
    dissatisfaction is that workers in larger agencies are
       A. less likely to be known to management and to be
          personally disciplined if they expressed dissatis-
          faction with their new roles
       B. less likely to have the opportunity to participate
          in planning a reorganization and to be given consi-
          deration for the assignments they preferred
       C. given a shorter lead period to implement the change
          and, therefore, had insufficient time to plan the
          reorganization and carry it out efficiently
       D. usually made up of more older members who have had
          routinized their work according to habit and find
          it more difficult to adjust to change

16. An article which recently appeared in a professional   16.___
    journal presents a proposal for participatory leadership
    in which the goal of supervision would be development of
    subordinates' self-reliance, with the premise that each
    staff member is held accountable for his own performance.
    The one of the following which would NOT be a desirable
    outcome of this type of supervision is the
       A. necessity for subordinates to critically examine
          their performance
       B. development by some subordinates of skills not
          possessed by the supervisor
       C. establishment of a quality control unit for sample
          checking and identification of errors
       D. relaxation of demands made on the supervisor

17. The *management by objectives* concept is a major develop- 17.___
    ment in the administration of human services organizations.
    The purpose of this approach is to establish a system for
       A. reduction of waiting time
       B. planning and controlling work output
       C. consolidation of organizational units
       D. work measurement

18. Assume that you encounter a serious administrative
    problem in implementing a new program. After consulting
    with members of your staff individually, you come up with
    several alternate solutions.
    Of the following, the procedure which would be MOST
    appropriate for evaluating the relative merits of each
    solution would be to
    A. try all of them on a limited experimental basis
    B. break the problem down into its component parts and
       analyze the effect of each solution on each component
       in terms of costs and benefits
    C. break the problem down into its component parts,
       eliminate all intangibles, and measure the effect of
       the tangible aspects of each solution on each com-
       ponent in terms of costs and benefits
    D. bring the matter before your weekly staff conference,
       discuss the relative merits of each alternate solu-
       tion, and then choose the one favored by the majority
       of the conference

18.___

19. When establishing planning objectives for a service
    program under your supervision, the one of the following
    principles which should be followed is that objectives
    A. are rarely verifiable if they are qualitative
    B. should be few in number and of equal importance
    C. should cover as many of the activities of the program
       as possible
    D. should be set in the light of assumptions about
       future funding

19.___

20. Assume that you have been assigned responsibility for
    coordinating various aspects of the case aide program in
    a community social services center.
    Which of the following administrative concepts would NOT
    be applicable to this assignment?
    A. Functional job analysis
    B. Peer group supervision
    C. Differential use of staff
    D. Systems design

20.___

21. Good administrative practice includes the use of outside
    consultants as effective technique in achieving agency
    objectives.
    However, the one of the following which would NOT be an
    appropriate role for the consultant is
    A. provision of technical or professional expertise not
       otherwise available in the agency
    B. administrative direction of a new program activity
    C. facilitating coordination and communication among
       agency staff
    D. objective measurement of the effectiveness of agency
       services

21.___

22. Of the following, the MOST common fault of recent research 22.___
projects attempting to measure the effectiveness of social
programs has been their
    A. questionable methodology B. inaccurate findings
    C. unrealistic expectations D. lack of objectivity

23. One of the most difficult tasks of supervision in a 23.___
modern public agency is teaching workers to cope with the
hostile reactions of clients.
In order to help the disconcerted worker analyze and
understand a client's hostile behavior, the supervisor
should FIRST
    A. encourage the worker to identify with the client's
       frustrations and deprivations
    B. give the worker a chance to express and accept his
       feelings about the client
    C. ask the worker to review his knowledge of the client
       and his circumstances
    D. explain to the worker that the client's anger is not
       directed at the worker personally

24. Determination of the level of participation, or how much 24.___
of the public should participate in a given project, is
a vital step in community organization.
In order to make this determination, the FIRST action
that should be taken is to
    A. develop the participants
    B. fix the goals of the project
    C. evaluate community interest in the project
    D. enlist the cooperation of community leaders

25. The one of the following which would be the MOST critical 25.___
factor for successful operation of a decentralized system
of social programs and services is
    A. periodic review and evaluation of services delivered
       at the community level
    B. transfer of decision-making authority to the community
       level wherever feasible
    C. participation of indigenous non-professionals in
       service delivery
    D. formulation of quantitative plans for dealing with
       community problems wherever feasible

KEY (CORRECT ANSWERS)

1. A	6. D	11. A	16. D	21. B
2. A	7. A	12. C	17. B	22. C
3. C	8. A	13. D	18. C	23. B
4. C	9. B	14. A	19. D	24. B
5. B	10. B	15. B	20. B	25. B

EXAMINATION SECTION

TEST 1

DIRECTIONS: Each question or incomplete statement is followed by several suggested answers or completions. Select the one that BEST answers the question or completes the statement. *PRINT THE LETTER OF THE CORRECT ANSWER IN THE SPACE AT THE RIGHT.*

1. The MAJOR responsibility of a director is to
   A. make certain that his line supervisors keep proper control of staff activity
   B. see that training is given to his staff according to individual needs
   C. insure that his total organization is coordinated toward agency goals and objectives
   D. work constructively with groups so that programs will reflect their needs

   1.___

2. A good organization chart of a department is an IMPORTANT instrument because it can
   A. make it easier to understand the mission of the department
   B. help new employees become acquainted with department personnel
   C. clarify relationships and responsibilities of the various department components
   D. simplify the task of *going to the top*

   2.___

3. Unnecessary and obsolete forms can be eliminated MOST effectively by
   A. appointing a representative committee to review and evaluate all forms in relation to operating procedures
   B. discarding all forms which have not been used during the past year
   C. assembling all forms and destroying those which are duplicates or obsolete
   D. directing office managers to review the forms to determine which should be revised or abolished

   3.___

4. The director must adopt methods and techniques to insure that his budgeted allowances are properly spent and that organizational objectives are being reached.
   These responsibilities can be fulfilled BEST by
   A. controlling operations with electronic data processing equipment
   B. shifting caseload controls from caseworkers to clerical staff
   C. installing a work simplification program and establishing controls for crucial areas of operation
   D. assigning employees with special skills and training to perform the more important and specialized jobs

   4.___

5. The MOST appropriate technique for making the staff   5.___
   thoroughly familiar with departmental policies would be to
   A. maintain an up-to-date loose-leaf binder of written
      policies in a central point in the office
   B. issue copies of all policy directives to the unit
      supervisors
   C. distribute copies of policy directives to the entire
      staff and arrange for follow-up discussion on a unit
      basis
   D. discuss all major policy directives at an office-wide
      staff meeting

6. When a proposed change in a departmental procedure is being   6.___
   evaluated, the factor which should be considered MOST
   important in reaching the decision is the
   A. extent of resistance anticipated from members of the
      staff
   B. personnel needed to execute the proposed change
   C. time required for training staff in the revised procedure
   D. degree of organizational dislocation compared with gains
      expected from the change

7. A director anticipates that certain aspects of a new   7.___
   departmental procedure will be distasteful to many staff
   members.
   Assuming that the procedure is basically sound in spite of
   this drawback, the BEST approach for the director to take
   with his staff is to
   A. advise them to accept the procedure since it has the
      support of the highest authorities in the department
   B. point out that other procedures which were resisted
      initially have come to be accepted in time
   C. challenge staff members to suggest another procedure
      which will accomplish the same purpose better
   D. ask the staff members to discuss the *pros* and *cons* of
      the procedure and suggest how it can be improved

8. At a staff meeting at which a basic change in departmental   8.___
   procedure is to be announced, a director begins the
   discussion by asking the participants for criticisms of the
   existing procedure. He then describes the new procedure to
   be employed and explains the improvements that are anticipated.
   The director's method of introducing the change is
   A. *good*, mainly because the participants would be more
      receptive to the new procedure if they understood the
      inadequacies of the old one
   B. *good*, mainly because the participants' comments on the
      old procedure will provide the basis for evaluation of
      the feasibility of the new one
   C. *bad*, mainly because the participants will realize that
      the decision for change has been made before the meeting,
      without consideration of the participants' comments
   D. *bad*, mainly because the discussion is focused on the old
      procedure, rather than on the procedure being introduced

9. Assume that you are conducting a staff conference to
   discuss the development of a procedure implementing a
   change in state policy. There are twelve participants
   whose office titles range from unit supervisor to senior
   supervisor, each of whom has responsibility for some
   aspect of the program affected by the policy change.
   After some introductory remarks, the BEST procedure for
   you to follow is to call upon the participants in the order
   of their

    A. titles, with the highest titles first because they are
   likely to have the most experience and knowledge of
   the subject

    B. titles, with the lower titles first because they are
   likely to be less inhibited if they are permitted to
   give their views before the senior participants speak

    C. places around the table, to promote informality and
   democratic procedure

    D. specialized knowledge of the subject so that those
   with the most knowledge and competence may lead the
   discussion

9._____

10. A staff member has suggested a way of reducing the time
    required to prepare a monthly report by combining several
    items of information, separating one item into two parts,
    and generally revising definitions of terms.
    The CHIEF disadvantage of such a revision is that

    A. comparison of present with past periods will be more
   difficult

    B. subordinates who prepare the report will require
   retraining

    C. forms currently in use will have to be discarded

    D. employees using the records will be confused by the
   changes

10._____

11. Assume that a director happens to be present at a regular
    staff conference conducted by a senior supervisor. During
    the course of the conference, the director frequently takes
    over the discussion in order to amplify remarks made by the
    supervisor, to impart information about departmental policies,
    and to modify or correct possible misinterpretations of the
    supervisor's remarks.
    The director's actions in this situation are

    A. *proper*, mainly because the conference members were
   given the latest and most accurate information concerning departmental policies

    B. *proper*, mainly because the director has an obligation
   to assist and support the supervisor

    C. *improper*, mainly because the director did not
   completely take over the conference

    D. *improper*, mainly because the supervisor was put in a
   difficult position in the presence of his staff

11._____

12. A center has a serious staff morale problem because of   12.___
    rumors that it will probably be abolished. To handle
    this situation, the director adopts a policy of promptly
    corroborating rumors that he knows to be true and denying
    false ones.
    Although this method of dealing with the situation should
    have some good results, its CHIEF weakness is that
    A. it *chases* the rumors instead of forestalling them by
       giving correct information concerning the center's
       future
    B. the director may not have the necessary information
       at hand
    C. status is given to the rumors as a result of the
       attention paid to them
    D. the director may inadvertently divulge confidential
       information

13. Realizing the importance of harmonious staff relationships, 13.___
    one of your supervisors makes a practice of unobtrusively
    intervening in any conflict situation among staff members.
    Whenever friction seems to be developing, he attempts to
    soothe ruffled feelings and remove the source of difficulty
    by such methods as rescheduling, reassigning personnel,
    etc. His efforts are always behind the scenes and unknown
    to the personnel involved.
    This practice may produce some good results, but the CHIEF
    drawback is that it
    A. permits staff to engage in unacceptable practices
       without correction
    B. violates the principle of chain of command
    C. involves the supervisor in personal relationships
       which are not properly his concern
    D. requires confidential sources of information about
       personal relationships within the center

14. Assume that the department adopts a policy of transferring   14.___
    administrative personnel from one center to another after
    stated periods of service in a center, or in a central office.
    Of the following, the MAIN advantage of such a policy is
    that it helps
    A. prevent the formation of cliques among staff members
    B. key staff members keep abreast of new developments
    C. effect a greater utilization of staff members' special
       talents
    D. develop a broader outlook and loyalty to the department
       as a whole, rather than to one center

15. A delegation of union members meets with you in your role   15.___
    as director to discuss obtaining assistance for a group of
    strikers who live in the neighborhood covered by the center.
    In the course of discussion, you learn that the strike has
    been called by the local union against the explicit direc-
    tive of the national union's leadership.
    The MOST appropriate course of action for you to take in
    this instance is to advise the union committee

A. of your sympathy and assure them that individual
   applications from the strikers for assistance will
   receive priority
B. that if the strikers are in need, they will be able
   to receive assistance as long as they are on strike
C. that since the strike is illegal, none of the workers
   will be eligible for assistance
D. that there is no bar to any of the strikers receiving
   assistance provided they are in need and are ready
   and willing to accept other employment if offered

16. The quality control system is a management tool used to   16.___
    test the validity of the eligibility caseload.
    This system can be helpful to a director in the following
    ways, with the EXCEPTION of
    A. obtaining objective data to use in evaluating the
       performance of specific staff members
    B. identifying the need for policy changes
    C. sorting out the source of errors in determining
       eligibility
    D. setting up training objectives for his staff

17. As director, you observe that there has been a sharp rise   17.___
    in the number of fair hearings. The increase seems to
    coincide with the intensified activities of the local
    recipients' organization.
    The MOST appropriate action under the circumstances is to
    A. determine whether the fair hearing requests result
       from weaknesses in the center's operation, and remedy
       the causes, if feasible
    B. disregard the matter for the time being because
       complaints have been stirred up by an organized client
       group
    C. emphasize to your staff the importance of meeting
       client needs promptly in order to avoid fair hearing
       requests
    D. resolve the grievances with the leaders of the
       recipients' organization

18. As director, you receive notice of a fair hearing decision   18.___
    from the State Commissioner ordering you to restore assis-
    tance to a family. You are appalled by the order because
    the facts cited by the hearing officer are at complete
    variance with what actually occurred, according to your
    personal knowledge of the case.
    Of the following, the MOST appropriate course of action
    for you to take first is to
    A. point out to central office that the decision should
       be reconsidered and appropriately modified
    B. comply with the decision under protest because it is
       patently wrong
    C. recommend to central office that it consider court
       action through an Article 78 proceeding to correct
       the erroneous decision
    D. comply with the decision, although an order of the
       State Commissioner has no force and effect of law

19. In your capacity as director, you have received a copy   19.____
of the monthly statistical report issued by the department.
In reviewing the report, you note that your center is
showing a rise in caseload which is substantially higher
than the average rise throughout the city.
Which of the alternatives listed below would be MOST
appropriate in order to deal with this situation?
   A. Make plans to discuss the situation with central office
      so that appropriate corrective action can be taken on
      the basis of your consultation
   B. Collect necessary information and data about the
      operations of your center and the area it serves to
      determine the cause of the trend, and plan appropriate
      action on the basis of your findings
   C. Call a meeting of your unit supervisors in order to
      impress upon them the importance of more diligent
      efforts to assist clients
   D. Assume that the rise in caseload is an inevitable
      result of the substantial increase in unemployment,
      and take no immediate action

20. Of the following phases of a training program for adminis-   20.____
trative personnel, the one which is usually the MOST
difficult to formulate is the
   A. selection of training methods for the program
   B. obtaining of frank opinions of the participants as
      to the usefulness of the program
   C. chief executive officer's judgment as to the need
      for such a program
   D. evaluation of the effectiveness of the program

21. Assume that you are conducting a conference dealing with   21.____
problems of the center of which you are the director. The
problem being discussed is one with which you have had no
experience. However, two of the participants, who have
had considerable experience with it, carry on an extended
discussion, showing that they understand the problem
thoroughly. The others are very much interested in the
discussion and are taking notes on the material presented.
To permit the two staff members to continue for the length
of time allowed for discussion of the problem is
   A. *desirable*, chiefly because introduction of the material
      by the two participants themselves may encourage others
      to contribute their work experience
   B. *desirable*, chiefly because their discussion may be
      more meaningful to the others than a discussion which
      is not based on work experience
   C. *undesirable*, chiefly because they are discussing
      material only in light of their own experience rather
      than in general terms
   D. *undesirable*, chiefly because it would reveal your own
      lack of experience with the problem and undermine
      your authority with the staff

22. In dealing with staff members, it is a commonly accepted   22.___
principle that individual differences exist, suggesting
that employees should be treated in an unlike manner in
order to achieve maximum results from their work assignments.
This statement means MOST NEARLY that
    A. supervisors should be aware of the personal problems
       of their subordinates and make allowances for poor
       performance because of such problems
    B. standardized work rules are ineffective because of
       the different capabilities of employees to maintain
       such work rules
    C. employees' individual needs should be considered by
       their supervisors to the greatest extent possible,
       within the practical limitations of the work situation
    D. knowledge of general principles of human behavior is
       generally of little use to a supervisor in assisting
       him to supervise his subordinates effectively

23. A supervisor under your jurisdiction reports to you that   23.___
one of his subordinates has been taking unusually long
lunch hours, has been absent from work frequently, and
has been doing poorer work than previously.
The BEST procedure for you to follow FIRST is to advise
the supervisor to
    A. prefer charges against the employee
    B. arrange for a psychological consultation for the
       employee
    C. ascertain whether the employee is ill and, if so,
       arrange a medical examination for him
    D. have a private conversation with the employee to
       obtain more information about the reasons for his
       behavior

24. If the term *executive development* is defined as the   24.___
continuous, on-going, on-the-job process of constructing
plans to improve individuals in specific positions, both
for the purpose of present improvement as well as for any
future advancement which is envisaged for the employee,
it follows that the emphasis in an executive development
program should
    A. provide learning experiences through formal or informal
       classes, seminars, or conferences, for which the focus
       is on the function of the position
    B. be oriented to the individual participant and may
       include a host of planned activities, such as appraisal,
       coaching, counseling, and job rotation
    C. attempt to create needs, to awaken, enlarge, and
       stimulate the individual so as to broaden his outlook
       and potentialities as a human being
    D. insure that the individual is able to plan, organize,
       direct, and control operations in the bureau, division,
       or agency

25. Most psychologists agree that employees have a need for   25. ___
recognition for the work they perform.
Therefore, it can be concluded that
    A. employees should be praised every time they complete
a job satisfactorily
    B. praise is a more effective incentive to good perfor-
mance than is punishment
    C. administrative personnel should be aware that sub-
ordinates do not have needs similar to their own
    D. a formalized system of rewards and punishment is
better than no system at all, as long as there is a
built-in consistency in its administration

KEY (CORRECT ANSWERS)

1. C		11. D
2. C		12. A
3. A		13. A
4. C		14. D
5. C		15. D
6. D		16. A
7. D		17. A
8. C		18. A
9. D		19. B
10. A		20. D

21. B
22. C
23. D
24. B
25. B

TEST 2

1. Studies have shown that the MOST effective kind of safety   1.___
   training program is one in which the
   A. training is conducted by consultants who are expert
      in the nature of the work performed
   B. lectures are given by the top.executives in an agency
   C. employees participate in all phases of the program
   D. supervisors are responsible for the safety training

2. Of the following, the MOST effective method of selecting   2.___
   potential top executives would be
   A. situational testing which simulates actual conditions
   B. a written test which covers the knowledge required to
      perform the job
   C. an oral test which requires candidate to discuss
      significant aspects of the job
   D. a confidential interview with his former employee

3. With regard to staff morale, MOST evidence shows that   3.___
   A. employees with positive job attitudes always out-
      produce those with negative job attitudes
   B. morale always relates to the employee's attitude
      toward his working conditions and his job
   C. low morale always results in poor job performance
   D. high morale has a direct relationship to effective
      union leadership

4. Of the following groups of factors, the group which has   4.___
   been shown to be related to the incidence of job accidents
   is
   A. personality characteristics, intelligence, defective
      vision
   B. experience, fatigue, motor and perceptual speed
   C. coordination, fatigue, intelligence
   D. defective vision, motor and perceptual speed,
      intelligence

5. Executives who have difficulty making decisions when faced   5.___
   with a number of choices USUALLY
   A. have domestic problems which interfere with the
      decision-making process
   B. can be trained to improve their ability to make
      decisions
   C. are production-oriented rather than employee-centered
   D. do not know their jobs well enough to act decisively

6. Studies of disciplinary dismissals of workers reveal that   6.___
   A. the majority of employees were dismissed because of
      lack of technical competence
   B. the supervisors were unusually demanding of employee
      competence
   C. most employees were dismissed because of inability to
      work with their co-workers
   D. the chief executive set unrealistic standards of
      performance

7. One philosophy of assigning workers to a specific job is   7.___
   that the worker and his job are an integral unit.
   This means, MOST NEARLY, that the
   A. employee and the job may both require adjustment
   B. employee must meet all the specifications of the job
      as a prerequisite for employment
   C. employee's morale will be affected by his salary
   D. employee's job satisfaction has a direct effect on
      his emotional health

8. The statement that the supervisor and the administrator   8.___
   are the *primary personnel men* means, MOST NEARLY, that
   A. supervisors and administrators are more skilled in
      personnel techniques than are professional personnel
      technicians
   B. they are in the best position to implement personnel
      policies and procedures
   C. employees have more confidence in their supervisors
      and administrators than in the professional personnel
      administrator
   D. personnel administration is most effective when it
      combines both centralized and decentralized approaches

9. Administrators frequently have to interview people in   9.___
   order to obtain information. Although the interview is a
   legitimate fact-gathering technique, it has limitations
   which should not be overlooked.
   The one of the following which is an IMPORTANT limitation
   is that
   A. individuals generally hesitate to give information
      orally which they would usually answer in writing
   B. the material derived from the interview can usually
      be obtained at lower cost from existing records
   C. the emotional attitudes of individuals during an inter-
      view often affect the accuracy of the information given
   D. the interview is a poor technique for discovering how
      well clients understand departmental policies

10. Leadership styles have frequently been categorized as   10.___
    authoritarian, laissez-faire, and democratic.
    In general, management's reliance on leadership to produce
    desired results would be MOST effectively implemented through
    A. the laissez-faire approach when group results are
       desired
    B. the authoritarian approach in a benevolent manner when
       quick decisions are required

    C. the democratic approach, when quick decisions are
       unimportant
    D. all three approaches, depending upon circumstances

11. As director, you are responsible for enforcing a recently   11._____
established regulation which has aroused antagonism among
many clients.
You should deal with this situation by
    A. explaining to the clients that you are not responsible
       for making regulations
    B. enforcing the regulation but reporting to your superior
       the number and kind of complaints against it
    C. carrying out your duty of enforcing the regulation as
       well as you can without comment
    D. suggesting to your clients that you may overlook
       violations of the regulation

12. One of the observations made in a recent psychological   12._____
study of leadership is that the behavior of a new employee
in a leadership position can be predicted more accurately
on the basis of the behavior of the previous incumbent in
the post than on the behavior of the new employee in his
previous job.
The BEST explanation for this observation is that there
is a tendency
    A. for a newly appointed executive to avoid making basic
       changes in operational procedures
    B. to choose similar types of personalities to fill the
       same type of position
    C. for a given organizational structure and set of duties
       and responsibilities to produce similar patterns of
       behavior
    D. for executives to develop more mature patterns of
       behavior as a result of increased responsibility

13. A director finds that reports submitted to him by his   13._____
subordinates tend to emphasize the favorable and minimize
the unfavorable aspects of situations.
The MOST valid reason for this is that
    A. subordinates usually hesitate to give their supervisors
       an honest picture of a situation
    B. the director may not have been sufficiently critical
       of previous reports submitted by his subordinates
    C. subordinates have a normal tendency to represent them-
       selves and their actions in the best possible light
    D. many subordinates in the field have developed a
       tendency to understatement in the depiction of
       unfavorable situations

14. Effective delegation of authority and responsibility to   14._____
subordinates is essential for the proper administration
of a center. However, the director should retain some
activities under his direct control.
Of the following activities, the one for which there is
LEAST justification for delegation by the director to a
subordinate is one involving
    A. relationships with client groups

B. physical danger to clients
C. policies which are unpopular with staff
D. matters for which there are no established policies

15. According to the principle of *span of control*, there
should be a limited number of subordinates reporting to
one supervisor.
Of the following, the CHIEF disadvantage which may result
from the application of this principle is a reduction in the
   A. contact between lower ranking staff members and
      higher ranking administrative personnel
   B. freedom of action of subordinates
   C. authority and responsibility of subordinates
   D. number of organizational levels through which a
      matter must pass before action is taken

16. The CHIEF objection to a practice of decentralizing the
preparation and distribution of memoranda by bureaus,
rather than controlling distribution through central
office, is that it is LIKELY to result in
   A. overloading bureaus with a multiplicity of communications
   B. limited and specialized rather than broad and general
      viewpoints in the memoranda
   C. violation of the principle of unity of command
   D. unimportant information being communicated to all
      bureaus

17. A report has been completed by members of your staff. As
director, you have reviewed the report and feel that the
information revealed could be damaging to the department.
You find yourself in conflict in your multiple role as
director, as a professional, and as a citizen.
The one of the following actions which would be MOST
desirable for you to take FIRST would be to
   A. send a copy of the report to your supervisor and
      request an immediate conference with him
   B. instruct staff to re-check the report and defer
      issuance of the report until the findings are confirmed
   C. immediately share the report with your supervisors
      and your advisory committee
   D. file the report until your advisory committee makes
      a request for it

18. In order for employees to function effectively, they
should have a feeling of being treated fairly by management.
Which of the following general policies is MOST likely to
give employees such a feeling?
   A. An employee publication should be mailed directly to
      the home of each employee.
   B. Employee attitude surveys should be conducted at
      regular intervals.
   C. Employees should be consulted and kept informed on
      all matters that affect them.
   D. Employees should be informed when the press publishes
      statements of policy.

19. In order to give employees greater job satisfaction, some management experts advocate a policy of job enrichment. The one of the following which would be the BEST example of job enrichment is to
    A. allow an aide to decide which portion of his normal duties and responsibilities he prefers
    B. increase the fringe benefits currently available to paraprofessional employees
    C. add variety to the duties of an employee
    D. permit more flexible working schedules for professional employees

19.___

20. Management of large organizations has often emphasized high salaries and fringe benefits as the most important means of motivating employees.
    The one of the following which is NOT an argument used to support this approach is
    A. most people endure work mainly in order to collect the rewards and to have the opportunity to enjoy them
    B. material incentives have proved to be the best means of stimulating creative capacity and the will to work
    C. the majority of employees place little emphasis on work-centered motivation to perform
    D. numerous research studies have shown that pay ranks first on a scale of factors motivating employees in government and industry in the United States

20.___

21. Some organizations provide psychologists or other professionally trained persons with whom employees can consult on a confidential basis regarding personal problems. Of the following, which is MOST likely to be a benefit management can derive from such a practice?
    A. Increase in the authority of management
    B. Disclosure of the corrupt practices of those handling money
    C. Receipt of new ideas and approaches to organizational problems
    D. Obtaining tighter control on employees' private behavior

21.___

22. Authorities agree that it is generally most desirable for an employee experiencing mental health problems to seek competent professional help without being required or forced to do so by another person.
    They view self-referral as a most desirable action PRIMARILY because
    A. it shows that the employee probably is more aware of the problem and more highly motivated to solve his problems
    B. the employee's right to privacy in his personal affairs is maintained
    C. another person cannot be blamed in the event the outcome of the referral is not successful
    D. the employee knows best his problems and will do what is necessary to serve his own best interests

22.___

Questions 23-25.

DIRECTIONS: Questions 23 through 25 consist of three excerpts
each. Consider an excerpt correct if all the
statements in the excerpt are correct.
Mark your answer as follows:
A. if only excerpts 1 and 2 are correct
B. if only excerpts 2 and 3 are correct
C. if only excerpt 1 is correct
D. if only excerpt 2 is correct

23. 1. Many executive decisions are based on assumptions.   23.___
        They may be assumptions supported by sketchy data about
        future needs for services; assumptions about the
        attitudes and future behavior of employees, perhaps
        based on reports of staff members or hearsay evidence;
        or assumptions about agency values that are as much a
        reflection of personal desires as of agency goals.
     2. A good pattern of well-conceived plans is only a first
        step in administration. The administrator must also
        create an organization to formulate and carry out such
        plans. Resources must be assembled; supervision of
        actual operations is necessary; and before the executive's
        task is completed, he must exercise control.
     3. When a problem is well defined, good alternatives identi-
        fied, and the likely consequences of each alternative
        forecast as best we can, one can assume that the final
        choice of action to be taken would be easy, if not
        obvious.

24. 1. Principles of motivation are not difficult to establish   24.___
        because human behavior is not complex and is easily
        understood; individual differences in human beings are
        substantial; and people are continuously learning and
        changing.
     2. What gives employees satisfaction or dissatisfaction
        indicates the nature of the motivation problem and
        provides positive guidance to the administrator who
        faces the problem of trying to get people to carry out
        a set of plans.
     3. The administrator's job of motivation can be described
        as that of creating a situation in which actions that
        provide net satisfaction to individual members of the
        enterprise are at the same time actions that make
        appropriate contributions toward the objectives of the
        enterprise.

25. 1. Administrative organization is primarily concerned   25.___
        with legal, technical, or ultimate authority; the
        operational authority relationships that may be created
        by organization are of major significance.
     2. Accountability is not removed by delegation. Appraisal
        of results should be tempered by the extent to which an
        administrator must rely on subordinates.

3. In delegations to operating subordinates, authority to plan exceeds authority to do, inasmuch as the executive typically reserves some of the planning for himself.

KEY (CORRECT ANSWERS)

1. C		11. B
2. A		12. C
3. B		13. C
4. B		14. D
5. B		15. A
6. C		16. A
7. A		17. D
8. B		18. C
9. C		19. C
10. D		20. D

21. C
22. A
23. A
24. B
25. D

READING COMPREHENSION
UNDERSTANDING AND INTERPRETING WRITTEN MATERIAL
EXAMINATION SECTION
TEST 1

DIRECTIONS: Each question or incomplete statement is followed by several suggested answers or completions. Select the one that BEST answers the question or completes the statement. *PRINT THE LETTER OF THE CORRECT ANSWER IN THE SPACE AT THE RIGHT.*

Questions 1-5.

DIRECTIONS: Questions 1 through 5 are to be answered SOLELY on the basis of the following paragraph.

There are several different schools of thought about the causes of juvenile delinquency. According to the *cultural-transmission* school of thought, delinquency is neither inborn nor developed independently. Children learn to become delinquents as members of groups in which delinquent conduct is already established and *the thing to do.* This school maintains that a child need not be different from other children or have any problems or defects of personality or intelligence in order to become a delinquent. On the other hand, the *psychogenic* school views delinquency as a method of coping with some underlying problem of adjustment. This school also holds that the tendency to become delinquent is not inherited. The delinquent, however, has frustrations, deprivations, insecurities, anxieties, guilt feelings, or mental conflicts which differ in kind or degree from those of non-delinquent children. Delinquency is thought of as a symptom of the underlying problem of adjustment in the same way as a fever is a symptom of an underlying infection. According to this school, if other children exhibit the same behavior, it is because they have independently found a similar solution to their problems.

1. Of the following, the MOST suitable title for the above paragraph would be   1.___
   A. PROBLEMS IN THE SCIENTIFIC STUDY OF JUVENILE DELIN-
      QUENCY
   B. THE EFFECT OF DISTURBED FAMILY SITUATION
   C. TWO THEORIES OF JUVENILE DELINQUENCY
   D. SOLUTIONS TO A MAJOR SOCIAL PROBLEM

2. According to the above paragraph, the *cultural-transmission*   2.___
   school of thought holds that there is a definite relationship between juvenile delinquency and the youths'
   A. intelligence   B. psychological problems
   C. family problems   D. choice of friends

3. According to the above paragraph, of the following, both   3.___
   schools of thought reject as a cause of juvenile delinquency the factor of
   A. guilt feelings   B. inherited traits
   C. repeated frustration D. extreme insecurities

4. On the basis of the above paragraph, which of the follow-   4.___
   ing statements is CORRECT?
   A. The *cultural-transmission* school of thought maintains
      that a child independently develops delinquent
      behavior as a solution to his problems.
   B. The *psychogenic* school of thought holds that children
      become delinquents because it is *the thing to do*.
   C. The *cultural-transmission* school of thought maintains
      that delinquency is the visible symptom of an under-
      lying personality problem.
   D. The *psychogenic* school of thought holds that delin-
      quents have mental conflicts that differ in kind or
      degree from non-delinquents.

5. The author's attitude toward these schools of thought is   5.___
   that he
   A. describes them objectively without indicating parti-
      ality to either school of thought
   B. favors the *cultural-transmission* school of thought
   C. favors the *psychogenic* school of thought
   D. suggests that he thinks both schools of thought are
      incorrect

Questions 6-7.

DIRECTIONS: Questions 6 and 7 are to be answered SOLELY on the
             basis of the following paragraph.

Behavior that seems strange to adults often is motivated by the
child's desire to please his peers or to gain their attention. His
feelings when ridiculed by his peers may range from grief to rage.
It is difficult for the child to express such feelings and the
reasons for them to adults for to do so he must admit to himself
the bitter fact that persons whose friendship he wants really do
not like him. Instead of directly expressing his feelings, he may
reveal them through symptoms such as fault-finding, fighting back,
and complaining. As a result, adults may not realize that when he
is telling them how much he dislikes certain children, he may really
be expressing how much he would like to be liked by these same
children, or how deeply he feels contempt of himself.

6. This paragraph implies that a child's constant complaints   6.___
   about certain other children may be his way of expressing
   A. his desire to be accepted by them
   B. his dislike of the adults around him
   C. ridicule for those he does not like
   D. how many faults those other children have

7. According to the above paragraph, a child may find it   7.___
   difficult to express his grief at being rejected by his
   peer group because
   A. his rejection motivates him to behave strangely
   B. he knows that the adults around him would not under-
      stand his grief

C. he may not be able to admit the fact of his rejection
   to himself
D. his anger prevents him from expressing grief

Questions 8-9.

DIRECTIONS: Questions 8 and 9 are to be answered SOLELY on the
             basis of the following paragraph.

A very small child has no concept of right or wrong. However,
as soon as he is sufficiently developed to be aware of forces outside
himself, he will begin to see the advantage of behaving so as to win
approval and avoid punishment. If the parents' standard of behavior
is presented to the child in a consistent manner, the child will
begin to incorporate that standard within himself so that he feels
the urge to do what his parents want him to do, whether they are
there or not. Furthermore, he will feel uncomfortable doing what he
thinks is wrong even if there is no probability of discovery and
punishment. If the parents' standard of behavior is NOT consistent,
the child may grow up too confused to establish any ideal for himself.
We then have a youngster who truly does not know right from wrong.
He is in danger of having no firm standard of behavior, no conscience,
and no feeling of guilt in defying the established community pattern.

8. The author of the above passage implies that a child   8.___
    whose parents do NOT present him with a consistent
    standard of behavior
      A. will learn the difference between right and wrong
         when he is older
      B. may feel no guilt when committing delinquent acts
      C. will feel uncomfortable doing what he thinks is wrong
      D. is likely to establish his own ideal standards

9. The above paragraph implies that when a child feels the   9.___
    urge to do what his parents want him to do, even if they
    are not present, it means that the child
      A. sees the advantages of behaving so as to avoid punish-
         ment
      B. has no concept of right and wrong
      C. has begun to develop a conscience based on his
         parents' standard of behavior
      D. is afraid that his parents will find out if he
         misbehaves

Questions 10-13.

DIRECTIONS: Questions 10 through 13 are to be answered SOLELY on
             the basis of the information in the following passage.

NEW YORK CITY GANGS

City social work agencies and the police have been meeting at City Hall to coordinate efforts to defuse the tensions among teenage groups that they fear could flare into warfare once summer vacations begin. Police intelligence units, with the help of the District Attorneys' offices, are gathering information to identify gangs and their territories. A list of 3,000 gang members has already been assembled, and 110 gangs have been identified. Social workers from various agencies like the Department of Social Services, Neighborhood Youth Corps, and the Youth Board, are out every day developing liaison with groups of juveniles through meetings at schools and recreation centers. Many street workers spend their days seeking to ease the intergang hostility, tracing potentially incendiary rumors, and trying to channel willing gang members into participation in established summer programs. The city's Youth Services Agency plans to spend a million dollars for special summer programs in ten main city areas where gang activity is most firmly entrenched. Five of the *gang neighborhoods* are clustered in an area forming most of southeastern Bronx, and it is here that most of the 110 identified gangs have formed. Special Youth Services programs will also be directed toward the Rockaway section of Queens, Chinatown, Washington Heights, and two neighborhoods in northern Staten Island noted for a lot of motorcycle gang activity. Some of these programs will emphasize sports and recreation, others vocational guidance or neighborhood improvement, but each program will be aimed at benefiting all youngsters in the area. Although none of the money will be spent specifically on gang members, the Youth Services Agency is consulting gang leaders, along with other teenagers, on the projects they would like developed in their area.

10. The above passage states that one of the steps taken by   10.___
   street workers in trying to defuse the tensions among
   teenage gangs is that of
   A. conducting summer school sessions that will benefit
      all neighborhood youth
   B. monitoring neighborhood sports competitions between
      rival gangs
   C. developing liaison with community school boards and
      parent associations
   D. tracing rumors that could intensify intergang
      hostilities

11. Based on the information given in the above passage on   11.___
   gangs and New York City's gang members, it is CORRECT to
   state that
   A. there are no teenage gangs located in Brooklyn
   B. most of the gangs identified by the Police are con-
      centrated in one borough
   C. there is a total of 110 gangs in New York City
   D. only a small percentage of gangs in New York City
      is in Queens

12. According to the above passage, one IMPORTANT aspect of   12.___
    the program is that
        A. youth gang leaders and other teenagers are involved
           in the planning
        B. money will be given directly to gang members for use
           on their projects
        C. only gang members will be allowed to participate in
           the programs
        D. the parents of gang members will act as youth leaders

13. Various city agencies are cooperating in the attempt to   13.___
    keep the city's youth *cool* during the summer school vaca-
    tion period.
    The above passage does NOT specifically indicate partici-
    pation in this project by the
        A. Police Department
        B. District Attorney's Office
        C. Board of Education
        D. Department of Social Services

Questions 14-16.

DIRECTIONS: Questions 14 through 16 are to be answered SOLELY on
              the basis of the following paragraph.

    Drug abuse prevention efforts are only in their beginning stages.
Far less is known about how to design programs that successfully
counter the seductive effects which drugs have upon the young than
about how to build clinics and programs to treat those who have become
addicts. The latter can be done with enough dollars, managerial
competence, and qualified personnel. The former depends upon such
intangibles as community leadership, personal attitudes, and, in the
final analysis, individual choices. Given this void in our society's
understanding of what it is that makes us so vulnerable to addiction,
government must build upon its growing experience to invest wisely in
those efforts that offer positive alternatives to drug abuse.

14. The one of the following which is probably the BEST title   14.___
    for the above paragraph is
        A. THE YOUTHFUL DRUG ABUSER
        B. GOVERNMENT'S MANAGEMENT OF DRUG PROGRAMS
        C. A SCIENTIFIC ANALYSIS OF DRUG CURES
        D. THE DIFFICULTY OF DRUG ABUSE PREVENTION

15. According to the above paragraph, treating drug addicts   15.___
    as compared to preventing drug addiction among the young
    is GENERALLY
        A. *easier*, mainly because there is more public interest
           in this method
        B. *harder*, mainly because qualified personnel are not
           readily available
        C. *easier*, mainly because there is more known about how
           to accomplish this objective
        D. *harder*, mainly because confirmed drug addicts do not
           give up the habit readily

16. According to the above paragraph, the role of government   16.___
    in dealing with the problem of drug addiction and youth
    should be to
        A. build larger clinics and develop additional programs
           for treatment of offenders
        B. help attract youth to behavior which is more desirable
           than that provided by the drug culture
        C. provide the funds and personnel essential to success-
           ful enforcement programs
        D. establish centers for the study and analysis of those
           factors that make our citizens vulnerable to addic-
           tion

Questions 17-20.

DIRECTIONS: Questions 17 through 20 are to be answered SOLELY on
             the basis of the following paragraph.

Many of our city's most troubled drug addicts are not being
reached by the existing treatment programs. They either refuse to
enter treatment voluntarily or have dropped out of these programs.
A substantial number of the city's heroin addicts, including some
of the most crime-prone, are unlikely to be reached by the mere
expansion of existing treatment programs.

17. According to the above paragraph, the drug addicts who   17.___
    have dropped out of existing programs
        A. are habitual criminals beyond hope of chance
        B. could be reached by expanding existing programs
        C. include the seriously disturbed
        D. had been compelled to enroll in such programs

18. According to the above paragraph, some drug addicts are   18.___
    not being aided by current treatment efforts because
    those addicts
        A. are serving excessively long prison sentences
        B. are unwilling to become involved in programs
        C. have been accepted by therapeutic communities
        D. have lost confidence in the city's programs

19. As used in the above paragraph, the underlined word prone   19.___
    means MOST NEARLY
        A. angered   B. bold   C. exclusive   D. inclined

20. As used in the above paragraph, the underlined word mere   20.___
    means MOST NEARLY
        A. formal   B. simple   C. remote   D. prompt

Questions 21-23.

DIRECTIONS: Questions 21 through 23 are to be answered SOLELY on the basis of the following passage.

A survey of the drinking behavior of 1,185 persons representing the adult population of Iowa in 1958 aged 21 years and older revealed that approximately 40 percent were abstainers. Of the nearly one million drinkers in the State, 47 percent were classed as light drinkers, 37 percent as moderate, and 16 percent as heavy drinkers. Twenty-two percent of the men drinkers were classed as heavy drinkers but only 8 percent of the women drinkers. The proportion of heavy drinkers increased with level of education among drinkers residing in the city - from 15 percent of the least educated to 22 percent of the most educated; but decreased among farm residents from 17 percent of the least educated to 4 percent of the most educated. Age differences in the extent of drinking were not pronounced. The age class of 36-45 had the lowest proportions of light drinkers, while the age class 61 and over had the lowest proportion of heavy drinkers.

21. According to the above passage, which one of the following   21.____
    statements concerning heavy drinking would be CORRECT?
    A. Experts are in sharp conflict regarding the reason
       for heavy drinking.
    B. The amount of heavy drinking in the city is directly
       proportional to the amount of education.
    C. The degree of heavy drinking is directly proportional
       to the age class of the drinkers.
    D. The degree of heavy drinking is inversely to the
       number of light drinkers.

22. Of the total drinking population in Iowa, how many were   22.____
    moderate drinkers?
       A. 370,000   B. 438   C. 370   D. 438,150

23. What percent of the men drinkers surveyed were NOT heavy   23.____
    drinkers?
       A. 60%   B. 84%
       C. 78%   D. Cannot be determined

Questions 24-25.

DIRECTIONS: Questions 24 and 25 are to be answered SOLELY on the basis of the following paragraph.

A drug-user does not completely retreat from society. While a new user, he must begin participation in some group of old users in order to secure access to a steady supply of drugs. In the process, his readiness to engage in drug use, which stems from his personality and the social structure, is reinforced by new patterns of associations and values. The more the individual is caught in this web of associations, the more likely it is that he will persist in drug use, for he has become incorporated into a subculture that exerts control over his behavior. However, it is also true that the resulting tics among addicts are not as strong as those among participants in criminal and conflict subcultures. Addiction is in many ways an individualistic adaptation for the *kick* is essentially a private experience. The compelling need for the drug is also a divisive force for it leads to intense competition among addicts for money. Forces of this kind thus limit the relative cohesion which can develop among users.

24. According to the above paragraph, the MAIN reason why new   24.___
    drug users associate with old users is a
       A. fear of the police
       B. common hatred of society
       C. need to get drugs
       D. dislike of being alone

25. According to the above paragraph, which of the following   25.___
    statements is INCORRECT?
       A. Drug users encourage each other to continue taking
          drugs.
       B. Gangs that use drugs are more cohesive than other
          delinquent gangs.
       C. A youth's desire to use drugs stems from his person-
          ality as well as the social structure.
       D. Addicts get no more of a *kick* from using drugs in
          a group than alone.

———

KEY (CORRECT ANSWERS)

1. C		11. B	
2. D		12. A	
3. B		13. C	
4. D		14. D	
5. A		15. C	
6. A		16. B	
7. C		17. C	
8. B		18. B	
9. C		19. D	
10. D		20. B	

21. B
22. A
23. C
24. C
25. B

TEST 2

DIRECTIONS: Each question or incomplete statement is followed by several suggested answers or completions. Select the one that BEST answers the question or completes the statement. *PRINT THE LETTER OF THE CORRECT ANSWER IN THE SPACE AT THE RIGHT.*

Questions 1-5.

DIRECTIONS: Questions 1 through 5 are to be answered SOLELY on the basis of the following passage.

In an attempt to describe what is meant by a delinquent subculture, let us look at some delinquent activities. We usually assume that when people steal things, they steal because they want them to eat or wear or otherwise use them; or because they can sell them; or even - if we are given to a psychoanalytic turn of mind - because on some deep symbolic level the things stolen substitute or stand for something unconsciously desired but forbidden. However, most delinquent gang stealing has no such utilitarian motivation at all. Even where the value of the object stolen is itself a motivating consideration, the stolen sweets are often sweeter than those acquired by more legitimate and prosaic means. In homelier language, stealing *for the hell of it* and apart from considerations of gain and profit is a valued activity to which attaches glory, prowess, and profound satisfaction.

Similarly, many other delinquent activities are motivated mainly by an enjoyment in the distress of others and by a hostility toward non-gang peers as well as adults. Apart from the more dramatic manifestations in the form of gang wars, there is keen delight in terrorizing *good* children and in driving them from playgrounds and gyms for which the gang itself may have little use. The same spirit is evident in playing hooky and in misbehavior in school. The teacher and her rules are not merely to be evaded. They are to be flouted.

All this suggests that the delinquent subculture is not only a set of rules, a design for living which is different from or indifferent to or even in conflict with the norms of the *respectable* adult society. It actually takes its norms from the larger culture but turns them upside down. The delinquent's conduct is right, by the standards of his subculture, precisely BECAUSE it is wrong by the standards of the larger culture.

1. Of the following, the MOST suitable title for the above   1.___
   passage is
   A. DIFFERENT KINDS OF DELINQUENT SUBCULTURES
   B. DELINQUENT HOSTILITY TOWARD NON-GANG PEERS
   C. METHODS OF DELINQUENT STEALING
   D. DELINQUENT STANDARDS AS REVEALED BY THEIR ACTIVITIES

2. It may be inferred from the above passage that MOST delin- 2.___
   quent stealing is motivated by a
   A. need for food and clothing
   B. need for money to buy drugs
   C. desire for peer-approval
   D. symbolic identification of the thing stolen with
      hidden desires

3. The passage IMPLIES that an important reason why delin- 3.___
   quents play hooky and misbehave in school is that the
   teachers
   A. represent *respectable* society
   B. are boring
   C. have not taught them the values of the adult society
   D. are too demanding

4. In the above passage, the author's attitude toward 4.___
   delinquents is
   A. critical   B. objective
   C. overly sympathetic   D. confused

5. According to the above passage, which of the following 5.___
   statements is CORRECT?
   A. Delinquents derive no satisfaction from stealing.
   B. Delinquents are not hostile toward someone without
      a reason.
   C. The common motive of many delinquent activities is
      a desire to frustrate others.
   D. The delinquent subculture shares its standards with
      the *respectable* adult culture.

Questions 6-8.

DIRECTIONS: Questions 6 through 8 are to be answered SOLELY on
             the basis of the following paragraph.

A fundamental part of the youth worker's role is changing the
interaction patterns which already exist between the delinquent group
and the representatives of key institutions in the community; e.g.,
the policeman, teacher, social worker, employer, parent, and store-
keeper. This relationship, particularly its definitional character,
is a two-way proposition. The offending youth or group will usually
respond by fulfilling this prophecy. In the same way, the delinquent
expects punishment or antagonistic treatment from officials and other
representatives of middle class society. In turn, the adult concerned
may act to fulfill the prophecy of the delinquent. Stereotyped
patterns of expectation, both of the delinquents and those in contact
with them, must be changed. The worker can be instrumental in
changing these patterns.

6. Of the following, the MOST suitable title for the above 6.___
   paragraph is
   A. WAYS TO PREDICT JUVENILE DELINQUENCY
   B. THE YOUTH WORKER'S ROLE IN CREATING STEREOTYPES

    C. THE YOUTH WORKER'S ROLE IN CHANGING STEREOTYPED
       PATTERNS OF EXPECTATION
    D. THE DESIRABILITY OF INTERACTION PATTERNS

7. According to the above paragraph, a youth who misbehaves   7.___
and is told by an agency worker that *his group is a menace
to the community* would PROBABLY eventually respond by
    A. withdrawing into himself
    B. continuing to misbehave
    C. making a greater attempt to please
    D. acting indifferent

8. In the above paragraph, the author's opinion about stereo-   8.___
types is that they are
    A. *useful*, primarily because they are usually accurate
    B. *useful*, primarily because they make a quick response
       easier
    C. *harmful*, primarily because the adult community will
       be less aware of delinquents as a group
    D. *harmful*, primarily because they influence behavior

Questions 9-15.

DIRECTIONS: Questions 9 through 15 are to be answered SOLELY on
the basis of the information in the following passage.

Laws concerning juveniles make it clear that the function of the
courts is to treat delinquents, not to punish them. Many years ago,
children were detained in jails or police lockups along with adult
offenders. Today, however, it is recognized that separate detention
is important for the protection of the children. Detention is now
regarded as part of the treatment process.

Detention is not an ordinary child care job. On the one hand, it
must be distinguished from mere shelter care, which is a custodial
program for children whose families cannot care for them adequately.
On the other hand, it must be distinguished from treatment in mental
health institutions, which is meant for children who have very serious
mental or psychological problems. The children in a detention facility
are there because they have run into trouble with the law and because
they must be kept in safe custody for a short period until the court
decides the final action to be taken in each child's case.

The Advisory Committee on Detention and Shelter Care has outlined
several basic objectives for a good detention service. One objective
is secure custody. Like adults who are being detained until their
cases come up before the court, children too will often want to escape
from detention. Security measures must be adequate to prevent ordinary
escape attempts, although at the same time a jail-like atmosphere
should be avoided. Another objective is to provide constructive
activities for the children and to give individual guidance through
casework and group sessions. A final objective is to study each child
individually so that useful information can be provided for court
action and so that the mental, emotional, or other problems that have
contributed to the child's difficulties can be identified.

9. According to the above passage, laws concerning juveniles   9.___
make it clear that the MAIN aim of the courts in handling
young offenders is to _____ juvenile delinquents.
   A. punish
   B. provide treatment for
   C. relieve the families of
   D. counsel families which have

10. The above passage IMPLIES that the former practice of   10.___
locking up juveniles along with adults was
   A. *good* because it was more efficient than providing
      separate facilities
   B. *good* because children could then be protected by the
      adults
   C. *bad* because the children were not safe
   D. *bad* because delinquents need mental health treatment

11. The above passage says that a detention center differs   11.___
from a shelter care facility in that the children in a
detention center
   A. have been placed there permanently by their families
      or by the courts
   B. come from families who cannot or will not care for
      them
   C. have serious mental or psychological problems
   D. are in trouble with the law and must be kept in safe
      custody temporarily

12. The above passage mentions one specific way in which   12.___
detained juveniles are like detained adults.
This similarity is that both detained juveniles and
detained adults
   A. may try to escape from the detention facility
   B. have been convicted of serious crimes
   C. usually come from bad family backgrounds
   D. have mental or emotional problems

13. The above passage lists several basic objectives that   13.___
were outlined by the Advisory Committee on Detention and
Child Care.
Which one of the following aims is NOT given in the list
of Advisory Committee objectives?
   A. Separating juvenile offenders from adult offenders
   B. Providing secure custody
   C. Giving individual guidance
   D. Providing useful information for court action

14. The above passage mentions a *custodial program*.   14.___
This means MOST NEARLY
   A. janitor services
   B. a program to prevent jail escapes
   C. caretaking services for dependent children
   D. welfare payments to families with children

15. The above passage says that *security measures* are needed   15.___
    in a detention center PRIMARILY in order to
    A. prevent unauthorized persons from entering
    B. prevent juveniles from escaping
    C. ensure that records are safeguarded for court action
    D. create a jail-like atmosphere

Questions 16-22.

DIRECTIONS: · Questions 16 through 22 are to be answered SOLELY on
           the basis of the following passage.

    Adolescents are among the last social groups in the world to be
given the full nineteenth-century colonial treatment. Our colonial
administrators, at least at the higher policymaking levels, are usually
of the enlightened sort who decry the punitive expedition except as an
instrument of last resort, though they are inclined to tolerate a shade
more brutality in the actual school or police station than the law
allows. They prefer, however, to study the young with a view to understanding them, not for their own sake but in order to learn how to
induce them to abandon their barbarism and assimilate the folkways of
normal adult life. The model emissary to the world of youth is no
longer the tough disciplinarian but the trained youth worker, who
works like a psychoanalytically oriented anthropologist. Like the
best of missionaries, he is sent to work with, and is aware and critical of the larger society he represents. But fundamentally, he accepts
it and often does not really question its basic value or its right to
send him to wean the young from savagery.

    The economic position of *the adolescent society*, like that of
other colonies, is highly ambiguous. It is simultaneously a costly
drain on the commonwealth and a vested interest of those members of
the commonwealth who earn their living and their social role by
exploiting it. Juvenile delinquency is destructive and wasteful, and
efforts to control and combat it are expensive. Schooling is even
more expensive. Both undertakings are justified on the assumption
that youth must be drawn into the social order if the social order is
to continue, and this is self-evident. But both act as agents of
society as it now is, propagating social values and assumptions among
a youth often cynical and distrustful but ignorant of the language or
the moral judgments in terms of which social complaints might be
couched. Neither the youth agency nor the school is usually competent
or sufficiently independent to help adolescents examine the sources
of their pain and conflict and think its meaning through, using their
continuing experience of life to help them build better social arrange-
ments in their turn. This, in a democracy, ought clearly to be among
the most fundamental functions of citizenship education; in a public
school system geared and responsive to local political demands and
interests, it may well be impossible. Official agencies dealing with
youth vary enormously in the pretexts and techniques with which they
approach their clientele, from those of the young worker attached to
a conflict gang to those of the citizenship education teacher in the
academic track of a suburban high school. But they all begin, like
a Colonial Office, with the assumption that the long-term interests of
their clientele are consistent with the present interests of their
sponsor.

16. The clientele and sponsor of official agencies dealing
    with youth are the
    A. young and the adult
    B. young and the educators
    C. educators and the young
    D. adult and the middle class

16.___

17. The author believes that the adolescent society is
    A. a drain on the commonwealth from which almost no one
       benefits
    B. the mainstay of the economy
    C. mercilessly exploited by certain adults
    D. costly to the government but a financial boon to
       certain adults

17.___

18. The author feels that society's present attempts to
    assimilate youth are motivated by
    A. greed
    B. a desire to end juvenile delinquency
    C. a desire to maintain the status quo
    D. a desire to induce the young to abandon their
       barbarism

18.___

19. The author is _____ society and _____ of youth.
    A. *approving* of present day; disapproving
    B. *approving* of present day; approving
    C. *disapproving* of adult; disapproving
    D. *disapproving* of adult; approving

19.___

20. According to the above passage, the BASIC function of
    citizenship education in a democracy ought to be to
    A. help adolescents examine the source of their pain
       and conflict
    B. help adolescents think the meaning of their problems
       through
    C. enable adolescents to perceive the meaning of
       experience
    D. enable adolescents to improve society through an
       understanding of their problems

20.___

21. The author is LEAST critical of
    A. nineteenth-century Colonialists
    B. the trained youth worker
    C. the members of the commonwealth who earn their living
       exploiting youth
    D. official agencies dealing with youth

21.___

22. It is implied in the above passage that
    A. colonialism is beneficial to the colonies
    B. society should not be stagnant but needs change
    C. society should have more effective ways of disciplin-
       ing recidivists
    D. youth is more interested in track than citizenship
       education

22.___

Question 23.

DIRECTIONS: Question 23 is to be answered SOLELY on the basis of the following passage.

Some adolescents find it very difficult to take the first step toward independence. Instead of experimenting as his friends do, a teenager may stay close to home, conforming to his parents' wishes. Sometimes parents and school authorities regard this untroublesome youngster with satisfaction and admiration, but they are wrong to do so. A too-conforming adolescent will not develop into an independent adult.

23. The above passage implies that a teenager who always 23.___ conforms to his parents' wishes
    A. should be admired by his teachers
    B. will develop into a troublesome person
    C. will become very independent
    D. should be encouraged to act more independently

Questions 24-25.

DIRECTIONS: Questions 24 and 25 are to be answered SOLELY on the basis of the following paragraph.

The skilled children's counselor can encourage the handicapped child to make a maximum adjustment to the demands of learning and socialization. She will be aware that the child's needs are basically the same as those of other children and yet she will be sensitive to his special needs and the ways in which these are met. She will understand the frustration the child may experience when he cannot participate in the simple activities of childhood. She will also be aware of the need to help him to avoid repeated failures by encouraging him to engage in projects in which he can generally succeed and perhaps excel.

24. According to the above paragraph, it is important for 24.___ the children's counselor to realize that the handicapped child
    A. should not participate in ordinary activities
    B. must not be treated in any special way
    C. is sensitive to the counselor's problems
    D. has needs similar to those of other children

25. According to the above paragraph, the counselor can BEST 25.___ help the handicapped child to avoid frustrating situations by encouraging him to
    A. participate in the same activities as *normal* children
    B. participate in activities which are not too difficult for him
    C. engage in projects which are interesting
    D. excel in difficult games

KEY (CORRECT ANSWERS)

1. D
2. C
3. A
4. B
5. C

6. C
7. B
8. D
9. B
10. C

11. D
12. A
13. A
14. C
15. B

16. A
17. D
18. C
19. D
20. D

21. B
22. B
23. D
24. D
25. B

PREPARING WRITTEN MATERIAL

PARAGRAPH REARRANGEMENT

COMMENTARY

The sentences which follow are in scrambled order. You are to rearrange them in proper order and indicate the letter choice containing the correct answer at the space at the right.

Each group of sentences in this section is actually a paragraph presented in scrambled order. Each sentence in the group has a place in that paragraph; no sentence is to be left out. You are to read each group of sentences and decide upon the best order in which to put the sentences so as to form as well-organized paragraph.

The questions in this section measure the ability to solve a problem when all the facts relevant to its solution are not given.

More specifically, certain positions of responsibility and authority require the employee to discover connections between events sometimes, apparently, unrelated. In order to do this, the employee will find it necessary to correctly infer that unspecified events have probably occurred or are likely to occur. This ability becomes especially important when action must be taken on incomplete information.

Accordingly, these questions require competitors to choose among several suggested alternatives, each of which presents a different sequential arrangement of the events. Competitors must choose the MOST logical of the suggested sequences.

In order to do so, they may be required to draw on general knowledge to infer missing concepts or events that are essential to sequencing the given events. Competitors should be careful to infer only what is essential to the sequence. The plausibility of the wrong alternatives will always require the inclusion of unlikely events or of additional chains of events which are NOT essential to sequencing the given events.

It's very important to remember that you are looking for the best of the four possible choices, and that the best choice of all may not even be one of the answers you're given to choose from.

There is no one right way to these problems. Many people have found it helpful to first write out the order of the sentences, as they would have arranged them, on their scrap paper before looking at the possible answers. If their optimum answer is there, this can save them some time. If it isn't, this method can still give insight into solving the problem. Others find it most helpful to just go through each of the possible choices, contrasting each as they go along. You should use whatever method feels comfortable, and works, for you.

While most of these types of questions are not that difficult, we've added a higher percentage of the difficult type, just to give you more practice. Usually there are only one or two questions on this section that contain such subtle distinctions that you're unable to answer confidently, and you then may find yourself stuck deciding between two possible choices, neither of which you're sure about.

EXAMINATION SECTION

DIRECTIONS: The sentences that follow are in scrambled order. You are to rearrange them in proper order and indicate the letter choice containing the correct answer. *PRINT THE LETTER OF THE CORRECT ANSWER IN THE SPACE AT THE RIGHT.*

PARAGRAPH REARRANGEMENT

1. (1) Nevertheless, management has devoted a good deal of attention to providing adequate ventilation, heat, and light; in general management attempts to insure working conditions that make a work-place physically satisfactory-- even attractive.
    (2) The objects of these needs include such things as food, drink, shelter, rent and exercise.
    (3) Our society is sufficiently prosperous, however, so that the minimum physiological requirements are usually met.
    (4) All human beings have needs that pertain to survival and physiological maintenance of the body.
    (5) Until such needs are reasonably well satisfied, they are strong, driving forces.
A. 4-2-5-3-1	B. 4-1-3-5-2
C. 3-4-1-2-5	D. 3-5-2-1-4

1.____

2. (1) As in direct-line relationships, a staff man probably consults with whomever he gives instructions to, and the man receiving the instructions may point out difficulties in execution to the staff man and to the line boss.
    (2) The most extreme formal technique for extending staff influence is the granting of functional authority.
    (3) This means that a staff man can give direct orders to operate personnel in his own name, instead of making recommendations to his boss or to other operating executives.
    (4) But until orders are recinded or revised, the company expects the worker to carry them out.
    (5) His instructions have the same force as those that come down the chain of command.
A. 1-3-4-2-5	B. 2-1-4-3-5
C. 2-3-5-1-4	D. 1-4-5-3-2

2.____

3. (1) Our capacity to rebuild the slums, to eliminate pollution, to give individuals an opportunity for self expression, to raise the standard of living, and to achieve our many other social and personal objectives rests on joint activity.
    (2) If individuals or even tribes attempt to be self-sufficient -- producing their own food, clothing and shelter -- subsistence is meager at best.
    (3) Modern man's aims and aspirations call for unprecedented cooperative effort.

3.____

(4) But when men join together in various enterprises,
pooling their resources and exchanging their outputs
with many other people or enterprises, they grasp the
means to flourish.
    A. 4-1-2-3   B. 3-1-2-4
    C. 1-3-4-2   D. 2-4-1-3

4. (1) Rather it is more constructive to list the types of   4.____
problems in the field and then decide how far we expect
a staff man to go in dealing with the problem.
(2) We can define the work of a staff man in terms of both
the subjects or problems he covers and what he does
about them.
(3) Unless a staff man, his boss, and everyone he works
with understand the scope of his work, his efforts may
cause more trouble then help.
(4) It is not enough, for example, for us to say that a
personnel director should handle staff services in the
field of personnel relations.
    A. 3-1-4-2   B. 4-3-2-1
    C. 1-2-3-4   D. 2-3-4-1

5. (1) These attacks come from a media which has no standards 5.____
for pre-entry testing, no code of ethics, no educational
requirements, and no oath to uphold.
(2) Yet we are asked to accept their professionalism.
(3) Recently, some members of the national media have taken
it upon themselves to recommend changes in the internal
management of law enforcement agencies.
(4) They have targeted on agencies which require graduate
degrees, sworn oaths of office, and adherence to high
ethical standards as minimum entry level requirements
for the privilege to serve.
    A. 3-4-1-2   B. 3-1-4-2
    C. 2-3-4-1   D. 3-2-1-4

6. (1) The concept of making optimum use of personnel re-   6.____
sources and coordination of the resources is called
"team police" approach.
(2) Overspecialization, however, is a deterrant to the
"team police" approach in larger departments because
specialists have a tendency to form elite groups within
the organization.
(3) All personnel are perceived as having a major contribution to make to the success of the organization.
(4) The approach removes all personnel from their nice neat
boxes which define specific and limited jobs, tasks, and
duties.
    A. 1-2-3-4   B. 4-3-2-1
    C. 1-4-3-2   D. 1-3-4-2

7. (1) People do not understand how difficult it is to be a   7.____
police officer.
(2) This sentiment is often expressed and deeply felt by
many police officers.

(3) Yet, for many reasons, such mutual understanding has been hard to achieve.

(4) Presumably, better police-public cooperation and accomodation would result if police were better able to communicate with citizens.

A. 1-2-3-4	B. 1-4-3-2
C. 1-2-4-3	D. 4-1-2-3

8. (1) But this is not the case.

(2) People in the work of administering criminal justice tend to see themselves in a profession which is static.

(3) Moreover, we tend to think of the criminal justice system as existing only in our time, and it is only an occasional reflection that makes us realize that we are only living in a small turn of the clock.

(4) We must be made to understand that there has been, is now, and always will be a behavior control system.

(5) Yet, as the present differs from the past, surely we must expect the future to be different also.

8.____

A. 1-3-4-2-5	B. 3-4-1-5-2
C. 2-3-1-4-5	D. 2-1-3-4-5

9. (1) A positive public image can help a department recruit and hold good personnel, maintain high morale, and gain public cooperation.

(2) One of the most important positions within a department for achieving these positive results is the uniformed patrol officer.

(3) His contacts with law-abiding citizens within the community may be the only contacts those citizens have with a member of the criminal justice system.

(4) It is necessary, therefore, for him to make a conscious effort to positively influence all those persons with whom he comes in contact during his routine daily activities.

9.____

A. 1-2-3-4	B. 2-3-4-1
C. 1-4-3-2	D. 4-1-2-3

10. (1) Such experiments are based on the recognition that typically the only meeting between the private citizen and the police is under circumstances of crises or confrontation where the policeman appears in only one segment of his role, and the citizen himself is likely to be out of character.

(2) Hopefully, the benefits of such exposure will be bilateral.

(3) Frequently, these efforts take the form of observational experiments whereby citizens are invited to observe the officers first hand as they carry out their duties.

(4) Increasing efforts have been made in recent years to overcome the often strained relationship between police officers and citizens.

10.____

(5) Whether expressed or not, the intent of experiments involving citizen observation of police work is to display the policeman to the public in a more total perspective.

    A. 1-5-3-4-2   B. 5-3-4-2-1
    C. 4-5-3-1-2   D. 4-3-1-5-2

11. (1) In recent years, partially as a result of the Women's Movement and law enforcement's shift to a more human-istic attitude and approach, the rape victim is begin-ning to receive different treatment.

    (2) These attacks on the criminal justice system have been sufficiently justified to result in the creation of new programs by law enforcement, and the passage of new laws by legislatures.

    (3) However, victims are starting to make their needs known, and the mistreatment they claim to have sometimes re-ceived from law enforcement and the criminal justice system has been chronicled by mass media.

    (4) At present, rape is the least reported and least punished of all felonies, with an estimated 70% to 90% of all rape cases going unreported.

    A. 1-2-3-4   B. 1-4-3-2
    C. 4-1-3-2   D. 1-3-4-2

11._____

12. (1) No one can be prepared for the psychological upheavals that may result.

    (2) Rape is a very traumatic experience.

    (3) However, many rape victims do experience some general reactions.

    (4) Law enforcement officers who deal with these victims should recognize and be aware of these reactions.

    A. 2-4-3-1   B. 2-1-3-4
    C. 4-2-1-3   D. 1-2-3-4

12._____

13. (1) One of the most common reactions to a forcible rape is an acute phase of disruption.

    (2) The victim seems completely out of control.

    (3) After this initial acute phase, there is a long term process wherein she attempts to re-integrate her dis-rupted life style.

    (4) During this re-integration period, it often appears that the woman has regained her equilibrium, but she has not.

    (5) The final phase is another period of adjustment when the woman's final level of equilibrium is reached.

    A. 1-2-3-4-5   B. 4-3-2-1-5
    C. 1-3-2-4-5   D. 3-2-1-4-5

13._____

14. (1) The average police department is too ingrown, too stag-nant, to undertake this kind of vigorous, sweeping action.

14._____

(2) For the development of truly efficient police forces, organized along functional lines requires the creation of new governmental structures; such an endeavor lies outside either the scope or the competence of the police.

(3) No matter what new models for the reform and reorganization of the police function are chosen, it is hardly realistic to expect that the initiative for these moves are to come solely, or perhaps even mainly, from within the police forces themselves.

(4) Nor, in a sense, is it fair to place the whole burden of reform on the shoulders of the police.

      A. 3-1-4-2   B. 4-2-1-3
      C. 3-2-4-1   D. 1-2-3-4

15. (1) These new technologies have had both positive and negative consequences, and for many of them, it has not yet even been possible to assess their consequences.

   (2) The twentieth century has witnessed an explosion of technologies as knowledge which has multipled itself several times over.

   (3) This has been an ever quickening cycle which has led man into entirely new dimensions of existence.

   (4) Added knowledge has enhanced technological capacities, and the advancing technologies have then contributed to the expanded existence of knowledge.

      A. 4-1-3-2   B. 3-1-4-2
      C. 2-4-3-1   D. 1-3-4-2

15._____

16. (1) This information, together with consideration of such factors as street design, degree of congestion, and natural barriers which might interfere with the assistance available from other police units, helps in determining the proper areas and times for one- or two-man patrol units.

   (2) Two-man cars are assigned to those areas and those periods of time where and when the frequency and nature of police activity justifies their use.

   (3) Consideration is given to the number of situations in which more than one person is arrested at a time; to the number of arrests involving resistance; and to the number of arrests involving the use of weapons.

   (4) The number of these incidents usually bears a direct relationship to the number of assaults, disturbances, and other acts of violence in a given area.

   (5) Also, the frequency of calls for police service will influence the decision to assign a two-man car.

      A. 4-2-1-3-5   B. 2-3-4-5-1
      C. 5-1-3-2-4   D. 3-4-5-2-1

16._____

17. (1) There is a little police officer in most everyone, which should be exploited by the police officer to the benefit of all.

   (2) The goal is to create the illusion that the witness and police officer are "working this case together as a team," while in reality the officer elicits the information he needs to pursue the investigation.

17._____

(3) A good interview technique to use with eyewitnesses at a crime scene is to make them feel that they are active participants in the investigation.
(4) Extreme formality should be avoided as it usually creates a barrier to effective communication.
    A. 4-1-3-2   B. 2-3-4-1
    C. 3-4-2-1   D. 3-1-4-2

18. (1) Moreover, a person feels immediately the rewards or punishments of his group, whereas benefits provided by a company for following its plan are usually more remote.
(2) If he deviates too far from group standards, other members may no longer want to associate with him and may treat him as though he were at least an oddball, if not a traitor.
(3) Such treatment is unpleasant even for those people who can move into other social groups.
(4) The pressure of a group on its members can be substantial, for an individual gets many of his satisfactions in his job through group responses.
    A. 4-2-3-1   B. 3-1-4-2
    C. 2-1-3-4   D. 1-3-4-2

18.____

19. (1) So, before we examine various means for engendering cooperation, the characteristics of a wholesome boss-subordinate relationship should be made clear.
(2) The need to build voluntary cooperation, instead of relying on power, calls for a fundamental shift in the way we think about leadership.
(3) Empathetic understanding, ego support, and provision of opportunities become central concepts.
(4) As we move away from power the nature of the interaction between boss and subordinate changes sharply.
    A. 1-4-3-2   B. 2-4-3-1
    C. 3-1-2-4   D. 4-1-2-3

19.____

20. (1) In simple situations, a supervisor watches work while it is being done.
(2) Each time a supervisor delegates work to a subordinate, he creates the problem of knowing whether the work is performed satisfactorily, and so delegating inevitably raises the question of control.
(3) For if a manager attempts to control the decisions of his subordinate, does he not repudiate his earlier delegation of planning?
(4) Then, when a large part of planning as well as operating is delegated, new complications are added.
(5) But when the delegated work increases, control by direct observations no longer remains possible.
    A. 4-3-5-2-1   B. 2-5-4-3-1
    C. 2-1-5-4-3   D. 1-3-5-2-4

20.____

21. (1) New medical research appears to strongly support this   21.____
        claim.
    (2) These products include such items as bread that is
        partly made of sawdust, and breakfast cereals that are
        85% sugar.
    (3) Yet people persist in putting every imaginable type of
        "food product" into their bodies.
    (4) Anthropologists have found that the phrase "you are what
        you eat" has existed for years in many cultures around
        the globe.
        A. 4-1-3-2   B. 3-2-1-4
        C. 4-3-2-1   D. 1-3-2-4

22. (1) For instance, plane fare is usually higher than bus or 22.____
        train fare, but one would probably incur fewer food and
        lodging expenses.
    (2) One should consider not only the actual cost of the
        different modes of transportation, but also the amount of
        time required to reach one's destination.
    (3) Thus, the overall cost of a long trip might be minimized
        by using the more expensive means of transportation.
    (4) Business travel should be accomplished in the most
        economical way.
        A. 1-2-3-4   B. 4-2-1-3
        C. 4-1-3-2   D. 2-4-3-1

23. (1) When these factors seem too overwhelming, "burnout"   23.____
        is the result.
    (2) Several factors might be involved.
    (3) "Burnout" describes a need to escape from a work situa-
        tion because the job is consuming too much of one's
        energy and life.
    (4) Lack of clarity around organizational and personal goals,
        uncertainty of rewards, lack of job security, lack of
        organizational and personal processes for saying "no,"
        and poor work habits all can contribute to an unsatisfying
        job situation.
        A. 3-2-4-1   B. 2-3-4-1
        C. 3-4-2-1   D. 1-3-4-2

24. (1) During the strike the workers received assistance from 24.____
        the IWW and financial support from outside sympathizers,
        such as Helen Keller.
    (2) In protest, the workers in the town struck the mills.
    (3) In 1912, textile operators responded to protective labor
        legislation that reduced the hours women could legally
        work by cutting wages.
    (4) The state's subsequent investigation of living and
        working conditions resulted in a report which touched
        on considerations central to an understanding of women
        as workers and strike leaders.
        A. 3-4-1-2   B. 3-2-1-4
        C. 3-1-4-2   D. 4-2-1-3

25. (1) Exposure to low doses of ionizing radiation can cause   25.___
        cancer twelve to forty years later and genetic disease
        and abnormalities in future generations.
    (2) Radiation harms human bodies by ionizing or altering the
        electrical charge of atoms and molecules that comprise the
        body's cells.
    (3) Even the smallest dose can affect us because the effects
        of radiation are cumulative.
    (4) Thus, there is no safe level of radiation.
                A. 3-4-1-2   B. 2-4-1-3
                C. 2-4-3-1   D. 2-3-1-4

———

KEY (CORRECT ANSWERS)

 1. A   11. B
 2. C   12. B
 3. B   13. A
 4. D   14. A
 5. A   15. C

 6. D   16. B
 7. C   17. D
 8. D   18. A
 9. A   19. B
10. C   20. C

        21. A
        22. B
        23. A
        24. B
        25. D

———

PHILOSOPHY, PRINCIPLES, PRACTICES, AND TECHNICS
OF
SUPERVISION, ADMINISTRATION, MANAGEMENT, AND ORGANIZATION

CONTENTS

CONTENTS (cont'd)

PHILOSOPHY, PRINCIPLES, PRACTICES, AND TECHNICS
OF
SUPERVISION, ADMINISTRATION, MANAGEMENT, AND ORGANIZATION

I. MEANING OF SUPERVISION

The extension of the democratic philosophy has been accompanied by an extension in the scope of supervision. Modern leaders and supervisors no longer think of supervision in the narrow sense of being confined chiefly to visiting employees, supplying materials, or rating the staff. They regard supervision as being intimately related to all the concerned agencies of society, they speak of the supervisor's function in terms of "growth", rather than the "improvement," of employees

This modern concept of supervision may be defined as follows:

Supervision is leadership and the development of leadership within groups which are cooperatively engaged in inspection, research, training, guidance and evaluation.

II. THE OLD AND THE NEW SUPERVISION

TRADITIONAL	MODERN
1. Inspection	1. Study and analysis
2. Focused on the employee	2. Focused on aims, materials, methods, supervisors, employees, environment
3. Visitation	3. Demonstrations, intervisitation, workshops, directed reading, bulletins, etc.
4. Random and haphazard	4. Definitely organized and planned (scientific)
5. Imposed and authoritarian	5. Cooperative and democratic
6. One person usually	6. Many persons involved (creative)

III. THE EIGHT (8) BASIC PRINCIPLES OF THE NEW SUPERVISION

1. *PRINCIPLE OF RESPONSIBILITY*

Authority to act and responsibility for acting must be joined.
   a. If you give responsibility, give authority.
   b. Define employee duties clearly.
   c. Protect employees from criticism by others.
   d. Recognize the rights as well as obligations of employees.
   e. Achieve the aims of a democratic society insofar as it is possible within the area of your work.
   f. Establish a situation favorable to training and learning.
   g. Accept ultimate responsibility for everything done in your section, unit, office, division, department.
   h. Good administration and good supervision are inseparable.

2. *PRINCIPLE OF AUTHORITY*

The success of the supervisor is measured by the extent to which the power of authority is not used.
   a. Exercise simplicity and informality in supervision.
   b. Use the simplest machinery of supervision.
   c. If it is good for the organization as a whole, it is probably justified.
   d. Seldom be arbitrary or authoritative.
   e. Do not base your work on the power of position or of personality.
   f. Permit and encourage the free expression of opinions.

3. *PRINCIPLE OF SELF-GROWTH*

The success of the supervisor is measured by the extent to which, and the speed with which, he is no longer needed.
   a. Base criticism on principles, not on specifics.
   b. Point out higher activities to employees.

c. Train for self-thinking by employees, to meet new situations.
d. Stimulate initiative, self-reliance and individual responsibility.
e. Concentrate on stimulating the growth of employees rather than on removing defects.

4. *PRINCIPLE OF INDIVIDUAL WORTH*
   Respect for the individual is a paramount consideration in supervision.
   a. Be human and sympathetic in dealing with employees.
   b. Don't nag about things to be done.
   c. Recognize the individual differences among employees and seek opportunities to permit best expression of each personality.

5. *PRINCIPLE OF CREATIVE LEADERSHIP*
   The best supervision is that which is not apparent to the employee.
   a. Stimulate, don't drive employees to creative action.
   b. Emphasize doing good things.
   c. Encourage employees to do what they do best.
   d. Do not be too greatly concerned with details of subject or method.
   e. Do not be concerned exclusively with immediate problems and activities.
   f. Reveal higher activities and make them both desired and maximally possible.
   g. Determine procedures in the light of each situation but see that these are derived from a sound basic philosophy.
   h. Aid, inspire and lead so as to liberate the creative spirit latent in all good employees.

6. *PRINCIPLE OF SUCCESS AND FAILURE*
   There are no unsuccessful employees, only unsuccessful supervisors who have failed to give proper leadership.
   a. Adapt suggestions to the capacities, attitudes, and prejudices of employees.
   b. Be gradual, be progressive, be persistent.
   c. Help the employee find the general principle; have the employee apply his own problem to the general principle.
   d. Give adequate appreciation for good work and honest effort.
   e. Anticipate employee difficulties and help to prevent them.
   f. Encourage employees to do the desirable things they will do anyway.
   g. Judge your supervision by the results it secures.

7. *PRINCIPLE OF SCIENCE*
   Successful supervision is scientific, objective, and experimental. It is based on facts, not on prejudices.
   a. Be cumulative in results.
   b. Never divorce your suggestions from the goals of training.
   c. Don't be impatient of results.
   d. Keep all matters on a professional, not a personal level.
   e. Do not be concerned exclusively with immediate problems and activities.
   f. Use objective means of determining achievement and rating. where possible.

8. *PRINCIPLE OF COOPERATION*
   Supervision is a cooperative enterprise between supervisor and employee.
   a. Begin with conditions as they are.
   b. Ask opinions of all involved when formulating policies.

        c. Organization is as good as its weakest link.
        d. Let employees help to determine policies and department
           programs.
        e. Be approachable and accessible - physically and mentally.
        f. Develop pleasant social relationships.

IV. WHAT IS ADMINISTRATION?

Administration is concerned with providing the environment, the material facilities, and the operational procedures that will promote the maximum growth and development of supervisors and employees. (Organization is an aspect, and a concomitant, of administration.)

There is no sharp line of demarcation between supervision and administration; these functions are intimately interrelated and, often, overlapping. They are complementary activities.

    1. *PRACTICES COMMONLY CLASSED AS "SUPERVISORY"*
        a. Conducting employees conferences
        b. Visiting sections, units, offices, divisions, departments
        c. Arranging for demonstrations
        d. Examining plans
        e. Suggesting professional reading
        f. Interpreting bulletins
        g. Recommending in-service training courses
        h. Encouraging experimentation
        i. Appraising employee morale
        j. Providing for intervisitation
    2. *PRACTICES COMMONLY CLASSIFIED AS "ADMINISTRATIVE"*
        a. Management of the office
        b. Arrangement of schedules for extra duties
        c. Assignment of rooms or areas
        d. Distribution of supplies
        e. Keeping records and reports
        f. Care of audio-visual materials
        g. Keeping inventory records
        h. Checking record cards and books
        i. Programming special activities
        j. Checking on the attendance and punctuality of employees
    3. *PRACTICES COMMONLY CLASSIFIED AS BOTH "SUPERVISORY" AND
       "ADMINISTRATIVE"*
        a. Program construction
        b. Testing or evaluating outcomes
        c. Personnel accounting
        d. Ordering instructional materials

V. RESPONSIBILITIES OF THE SUPERVISOR

A person employed in a supervisory capacity must constantly be able to improve his own efficiency and ability. He represents the employer to the employees and only continuous self-examination can make him a capable supervisor.

Leadership and training are the supervisor's responsibility. An efficient working unit is one in which the employees work with the supervisor. It is his job to bring out the best in his employees. He must always be relaxed, courteous and calm in his association with his employees. Their feelings are important, and a harsh attitude does not develop the most efficient employees.

VI. COMPETENCIES OF THE SUPERVISOR

1. Complete knowledge of the duties and responsibilities of his position.
2. To be able to organize a job, plan ahead and carry through.
3. To have self-confidence and initiative.
4. To be able to handle the unexpected situation and make quick decisions.
5. To be able to properly train subordinates in the positions they are best suited for.
6. To be able to keep good human relations among his subordinates.
7. To be able to keep good human relations between his subordinates and himself and to earn their respect and trust.

VII. THE PROFESSIONAL SUPERVISOR-EMPLOYEE RELATIONSHIP

There are two kinds of efficiency: one kind is only apparent and is produced in organizations through the exercise of mere discipline; this is but a simulation of the second, or true, efficiency which springs from spontaneous cooperation. If you are a manager, no matter how great or small your responsibility, it is your job, in the final analysis, to create and develop this involuntary cooperation among the people whom you supervise. For, no matter how powerful a combination of money, machines, and materials a company may have, this is a dead and sterile thing without a team of willing, thinking and articulate people to guide it.

The following 21 points are presented as indicative of the exemplary basic relationship that should exist between supervisor and employee:

1. Each person wants to be liked and respected by his fellow employee and wants to be treated with consideration and respect by his superior.
2. The most competent employee will make an error. However, in a unit where good relations exist between the supervisor and his employees, tenseness and fear do not exist. Thus, errors are not hidden or covered up and the efficiency of a unit is not impaired.
3. Subordinates resent rules, regulations, or orders that are unreasonable or unexplained.
4. Subordinates are quick to resent unfairness, harshness, injustices and favoritism.
5. An employee will accept responsibility if he knows that he will be complimented for a job well done, and not too harshly chastized for failure; that his supervisor will check the cause of the failure, and, if it was the supervisor's fault, he will assume the blame therefor. If it was the employee's fault, his supervisor will explain the correct method or means of handling the responsibility.
6. An employee wants to receive credit for a suggestion he has made, that is used. If a suggestion cannot be used, the employee is entitled to an explanation. The supervisor should not say "no" and close the subject.
7. Fear and worry slow up a worker's ability. Poor working environment can impair his physical and mental health. A good supervisor avoids forceful methods, threats and arguments to get a job done.
8. A forceful supervisor is able to train his employees individually and as a team, and is able to motivate them in the proper channels.

9. A mature supervisor is able to properly evaluate his subordinates and to keep them happy and satisfied.
10. A sensitive supervisor will never patronize his subordinates.
11. A worthy supervisor will respect his employees' confidences.
12. Definite and clear-cut responsibilities should be assigned to each executive.
13. Responsibility should always be coupled with corresponding authority.
14. No change should be made in the scope or responsibilities of a position without a definite understanding to that effect on the part of all persons concerned.
15. No executive or employee, occupying a single position in the organization, should be subject to definite orders from more than one source.
16. Orders should never be given to subordinates over the head of a responsible executive. Rather than do this, the officer in question should be supplanted.
17. Criticisms of subordinates should, whever possible, be made privately, and in no case should a subordinate be criticized in the presence of executives or employees of equal or lower rank.
18. No dispute or difference between executives or employees as to authority or responsibilities should be considered too trivial for prompt and careful adjudication.
19. Promotions, wage changes, and disciplinary action should always be approved by the executive immediately superior to the one directly responsible.
20. No executive or employee should ever be required, or expected, to be at the same time an assistant to, and critic of, another.
21. Any executive whose work is subject to regular inspection should, whever practicable, be given the assistance and facilities necessary to enable him to maintain an independent check of the quality of his work.

VIII. MINI-TEXT IN SUPERVISION, ADMINISTRATION, MANAGEMENT, AND ORGANIZATION

A. BRIEF HIGHLIGHTS

Listed concisely and sequentially are major headings and important data in the field for quick recall and review.

1. *LEVELS OF MANAGEMENT*

Any organization of some size has several levels of management. In terms of a ladder the levels are:

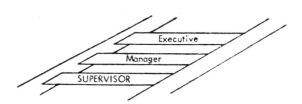

The first level is very important because it is the beginning point of management leadership.

2. *WHAT THE SUPERVISOR MUST LEARN*

A supervisor must learn to:
(1) Deal with people and their differences
(2) Get the job done through people
(3) Recognize the problems when they exist
(4) Overcome obstacles to good performance
(5) Evaluate the performance of people
(6) Check his own performance in terms of accomplishment

3. *A DEFINITION OF SUPERVISOR*
   The term supervisor means any individual having authority, in the interests of the employer, to hire, transfer, suspend, lay-off, recall, promote, discharge, assign, reward, or discipline other employees... or responsibility to direct them, or to adjust their grievances, or effectively to recommend such action, if, in connection with the foregoing, exercise of such authority is not of a merely routine or clerical nature but requires the use of independent judgment.

4. *ELEMENTS OF THE TEAM CONCEPT*
   What is involved in teamwork? The component parts are:

(1) Members	(3) Goals	(5) Cooperation
(2) A leader	(4) Plans	(6) Spirit

5. *PRINCIPLES OF ORGANIZATION*
   (1) A team member must know what his job is
   (2) Be sure that the nature and scope of a job are understood
   (3) Authority and responsibility should be carefully spelled out
   (4) A supervisor should be permitted to make the maximum number of decisions affecting his employees
   (5) Employees should report to only one supervisor
   (6) A supervisor should direct only as many employees as he can handle effectively
   (7) An organization plan should be flexible
   (8) Inspection and performance of work should be separate
   (9) Organizational problems should receive immediate attention
   (10) Assign work in line with ability and experience

6. *THE FOUR IMPORTANT PARTS OF EVERY JOB*
   (1) Inherent in every job is the *accountability* for results
   (2) A second set of factors in every job are *responsibilities*
   (3) Along with duties and responsibilities one must have the *authority* to act within certain limits without obtaining permission to proceed
   (4) No job exists in a vacuum. The supervisor is surrounded by key *relationships*

7. *PRINCIPLES OF DELEGATION*
   Where work is delegated for the first time, the supervisor should think in terms of these questions:
   (1) Who is best qualified to do this?
   (2) Can an employee improve his abilities by doing this?
   (3) How long should an employee spend on this?
   (4) Are there any special problems for which he will need guidance?
   (5) How broad a delegation can I make?

8. *PRINCIPLES OF EFFECTIVE COMMUNICATIONS*
   (1) Determine the media
   (2) To whom directed?
   (3) Identification and source authority
   (4) Is communication understood?

9. *PRINCIPLES OF WORK IMPROVEMENT*
   (1) Most people usually do only the work which is assigned to them
   (2) Workers are likely to fit assigned work into the time available to perform it
   (3) A good workload usually stimulates output
   (4) People usually do their best work when they know that results will be reviewed or inspected

6

(5) Employees usually feel that someone else is responsible for conditions of work, workplace layout, job methods, type of tools and equipment, and other such factors
(6) Employees are usually defensive about their job security
(7) Employees have natural resistance to change
(8) Employees can support or destroy a supervisor
(9) A supervisor usually earns the respect of his people through his personal example of diligence and efficiency

10. *AREAS OF JOB IMPROVEMENT*

The *areas* of job improvement are quite numerous, but the most common ones which a supervisor can identify and utilize are:

(1) Departmental layout   (5) Work methods
(2) Flow of work   (6) Materials handling
(3) Workplace layout   (7) Utilization
(4) Utilization of manpower   (8) Motion economy

11. *SEVEN KEY POINTS IN MAKING IMPROVEMENTS*

(1) Select the job to be improved
(2) Study how it is being done now
(3) Question the present method
(4) Determine actions to be taken
(5) Chart proposed method
(6) Get approval and apply
(7) Solicit worker participation

12. *CORRECTIVE TECHNIQUES OF JOB IMPROVEMENT*

Specific Problems	*General Problems*	*Corrective Technique*
(1) Size of workload	(1) Departmental layout	(1) Study with scale model
(2) Inability to meet schedules	(2) Flow of work	(2) Flow chart study
(3) Strain and fatigue	(3) Workplan layout	(3) Motion analysis
(4) Improper use of men and skills	(4) Utilization of manpower	(4) Comparison of units produced to standard allowances
(5) Waste, poor quality, unsafe conditions	(5) Work methods	(5) Methods analysis
(6) Bottleneck conditions that hinder output	(6) Materials handling	(6) Flow chart and equipment study
(7) Poor utilization of equipment and machines	(7) Utilization of equipment	(7) Down time vs. running time
(8) Efficiency and productivity of labor	(8) Motion economy	(8) Motion analysis

13. *A PLANNING CHECKLIST*

(1) Objectives   (8) Equipment
(2) Controls   (9) Supplies and materials
(3) Delegations   (10) Utilization of time
(4) Communications   (11) Safety
(5) Resources   (12) Money
(6) Methods and procedures   (13) Work
(7) Manpower   (14) Timing of improvements

14. *FIVE CHARACTERISTICS OF GOOD DIRECTIONS*

In order to get results, directions must be:

(1) Possible of accomplishment   (4) Planned and complete
(2) Agreeable with worker interests (5) Unmistakably clear
(3) Related to mission

15. *TYPES OF DIRECTIONS*
        (1) Demands or direct orders   (3) Suggestion or implication
        (2) Requests   (4) Volunteering

16. *CONTROLS*
    A typical listing of the overall areas in which the supervisor should establish controls might be:
        (1) Manpower   (4) Quantity of work (7) Money
        (2) Materials   (5) Time   (8) Methods
        (3) Quality of work (6) Space

17. *ORIENTING THE NEW EMPLOYEE*
        (1) Prepare for him   (3) Orientation for the job
        (2) Welcome the new employee (4) Follow-up

18. *CHECKLIST FOR ORIENTING NEW EMPLOYEES*

                                                      Yes No

        (1) Do your appreciate the feelings of new employees when they first report for work? ... ...

        (2) Are you aware of the fact that the new employee must make a big adjustment to his job? ... ...

        (3) Have you given him good reasons for liking the job and the organization? ... ...

        (4) Have you prepared for his first day on the job? ... ...

        (5) Did you welcome him cordially and make him feel needed? ... ...

        (6) Did you establish rapport with him so that he feels free to talk and discuss matters with you?... ...

        (7) Did you explain his job to him and his relationship to you? ... ...

        (8) Does he know that his work will be evaluated periodically on a basis that is fair and objective?.. ...

        (9) Did you introduce him to his fellow workers in such a way that they are likely to accept him? ... ...

     (10) Does he know what employee benefits he will receive? ... ...

     (11) Does he understand the importance of being on the job and what to do if he must leave his duty station? ... ...

     (12) Has he been impressed with the importance of accident prevention and safe practice? ... ...

     (13) Does he generally know his way around the department? ... ...

     (14) Is he under the guidance of a sponsor who will teach the right ways of doing things? ... ...

     (15) Do you plan to follow-up so that he will continue to adjust successfully to his job? ... ...

19. *PRINCIPLES OF LEARNING*
        (1) Motivation (2) Demonstration or explanation
        (3) Practice

20. *CAUSES OF POOR PERFORMANCE*
        (1) Improper training for job (6) Lack of standards of
        (2) Wrong tools   performance
        (3) Inadequate directions   (7) Wrong work habits
        (4) Lack of supervisory follow-up(8) Low morale
        (5) Poor communications   (9) Other

21. *FOUR MAJOR STEPS IN ON-THE-JOB INSTRUCTION*
        (1) Prepare the worker   (3) Tryout performance
        (2) Present the operation   (4) Follow-up

22. *EMPLOYEES WANT FIVE THINGS*
    (1) Security   (2) Opportunity   (3) Recognition
    (4) Inclusion   (5) Expression
23. *SOME DON'TS IN REGARD TO PRAISE*
    (1) Don't praise a person for something he hasn't done
    (2) Don't praise a person unless you can be sincere
    (3) Don't be sparing in praise just because your superior
        withholds it from you
    (4) Don't let too much time elapse between good performance
        and recognition of it
24. *HOW TO GAIN YOUR WORKERS' CONFIDENCE*
    Methods of developing confidence include such things as:
    (1) Knowing the interests, habits, hobbies of employees
    (2) Admitting your own inadequacies
    (3) Sharing and telling of confidence in others
    (4) Supporting people when they are in trouble
    (5) Delegating matters that can be well handled
    (6) Being frank and straightforward about problems and work-
        ing conditions
    (7) Encouraging others to bring their problems to you
    (8) Taking action on problems which impede worker progress
25. *SOURCES OF EMPLOYEE PROBLEMS*
    On-the-job causes might be such things as:
    (1) A feeling that favoritism is exercised in assignments
    (2) Assignment of overtime
    (3) An undue amount of supervision
    (4) Changing methods or systems
    (5) Stealing of ideas or trade secrets
    (6) Lack of interest in job
    (7) Threat of reduction in force
    (8) Ignorance or lack of communications
    (9) Poor equipment
    (10) Lack of knowing how supervisor feels toward employee
    (11) Shift assignments
    Off-the-job problems might have to do with:
    (1) Health   (2) Finances   (3) Housing   (4) Family
26. *THE SUPERVISOR'S KEY TO DISCIPLINE*
    There are several key points about discipline which the super-
    visor should keep in mind:
    (1) Job discipline is one of the disciplines of life and is
        directed by the supervisor.
    (2) It is more important to correct an employee fault than to
        fix blame for it.
    (3) Employee performance is affected by problems both on the
        job and off.
    (4) Sudden or abrupt changes in behavior can be indications of
        important employee problems.
    (5) Problems should be dealt with as soon as possible after
        they are identified.
    (6) The attitude of the supervisor may have more to do with
        solving problems than the techniques of problem solving.
    (7) Correction of employee behavior should be resorted to only
        after the supervisor is sure that training or counseling
        will not be helpful
    (8) Be sure to document your disciplinary actions.

(9) Make sure that you are disciplining on the basis of facts rather than personal feelings.

(10) Take each disciplinary step in order, being careful not to make snap judgments, or decisions based on impatience.

27. *FIVE IMPORTANT PROCESSES OF MANAGEMENT*

(1) Planning   (2) Organizing   (3) Scheduling
(4) Controlling   (5) Motivating

28. *WHEN THE SUPERVISOR FAILS TO PLAN*

(1) Supervisor creates impression of not knowing his job
(2) May lead to excessive overtime
(3) Job runs itself-- supervisor lacks control
(4) Deadlines and appointments missed
(5) Parts of the work go undone
(6) Work interrupted by emergencies
(7) Sets a bad example
(8) Uneven workload creates peaks and valleys
(9) Too much time on minor details at expense of more important tasks

29. *FOURTEEN GENERAL PRINCIPLES OF MANAGEMENT*

(1) Division of work   (8) Centralization
(2) Authority and responsibility (9) Scalar chain
(3) Discipline   (10) Order
(4) Unity of command   (11) Equity
(5) Unity of direction   (12) Stability of tenure of
(6) Subordination of individual   personnel
     interest to general interest(13) Initiative
(7) Remuneration of personnel   (14) Esprit de corps

30. *CHANGE*

Bringing about change is perhaps attempted more often, and yet less well understood, than anything else the supervisor does. How do people generally react to change? (People tend to resist change that is imposed upon them by other individuals or circumstances.)

Change is characteristic of every situation. It is a part of every real endeavor where the efforts of people are concerned.

A. Why do people resist change?

People may resist change because of:

(1) Fear of the unknown
(2) Implied criticism
(3) Unpleasant experiences in the past
(4) Fear of loss of status
(5) Threat to the ego
(6) Fear of loss of economic stability

B. How can we best overcome the resistance to change?

In initiating change, take these steps:

(1) Get ready to sell
(2) identify sources of help
(3) Anticipate objections
(4) Sell benefits
(5) Listen in depth
(6) Follow up

B. BRIEF TOPICAL SUMMARIES

I. WHO/WHAT IS THE SUPERVISOR?
   1. The supervisor is often called the "highest level employee and the lowest level manager."
   2. A supervisor is a member of both management and the work group. He acts as a bridge between the two.
   3. Most problems in supervision are in the area of human relations, or people problems.
   4. Employees expect: Respect, opportunity to learn and to advance, and a sense of belonging, and so forth.
   5. Supervisors are responsible for directing people and organizing work. Planning is of paramount importance.
   6. A position description is a set of duties and responsibilities inherent to a given position.
   7. It is important to keep the position description up-to-date and to provide each employee with his own copy.

II. THE SOCIOLOGY OF WORK
   1. People are alike in many ways; however each individual is unique.
   2. The supervisor is challenged in getting to know employee differences. Acquiring skills in evaluating individuals is an asset.
   3. Maintaining meaningful working relationships in the organization is of great importance.
   4. The supervisor has an obligation to help individuals to develop to their fullest potential.
   5. Job rotation on a planned basis helps to build versatility and to maintain interest and enthusiasm in work groups.
   6. Cross training (job rotation) provides backup skills.
   7. The supervisor can help reduce tension by maintaining a sense of humor, providing guidance to employees, and by making reasonable and timely decisions. Employees respond favorably to working under reasonably predictable circumstances.
   8. Change is characteristic of all managerial behavior. The supervisor must adjust to changes in procedures, new methods, technological changes, and to a number of new and sometimes challenging situations.
   9. To overcome the natural tendency for people to resist change, the supervisor should become more skillful in initiating change.

III. PRINCIPLES AND PRACTICES OF SUPERVISION
   1. Employees should be required to answer to only one superior.
   2. A supervisor can effectively direct only a limited number of employees, depending upon the complexity, variety, and proximity of the jobs involved.
   3. The organizational chart presents the organization in graphic form. It reflects lines of authority and responsibility as well as interrelationships of units within the organization.
   4. Distribution of work can be improved through an analysis using the "Work Distribution Chart."
   5. The "Work Distribution Chart" reflects the division of work within a unit in understandable form.
   6. When related tasks are given to an employee, he has a better chance of increasing his skills through training.
   7. The individual who is given the responsibility for tasks must also be given the appropriate authority to insure adequate results.
   8. The supervisor should delegate repetitive, routine work. Preparation of recurring reports, maintaining leave and attendance records are some examples.

11

9. Good discipline is essential to good task performance. Discipline is reflected in the actions of employees on the job in the absence of supervision.

10. Disciplinary action may have to be taken when the positive aspects of discipline have failed. Reprimand, warning, and suspension are examples of disciplinary action.

11. If a situation calls for a reprimand, be sure it is deserved and remember it is to be done in private.

IV. DYNAMIC LEADERSHIP

1. A style is a personal method or manner of exerting influence.

2. Authoritarian leaders often see themselves as the source of power and authority.

3. The democratic leader often perceives the group as the source of authority and power.

4. Supervisors tend to do better when using the pattern of leadership that is most natural for them.

5. Social scientists suggest that the effective supervisor use the leadership style that best fits the problem or circumstances involved.

6. All four styles -- telling, selling, consulting, joining -- have their place. Using one does not preclude using the other at another time.

7. The theory X point of view assumes that the average person dislikes work, will avoid it whenever possible, and must be coerced to achieve organizational objectives.

8. The theory Y point of view assumes that the average person considers work to be as natural as play, and, when the individual is committed, he requires little supervision or direction to accomplish desired objectives.

9. The leader's basic assumptions concerning human behavior and human nature affect his actions, decisions, and other managerial practices.

10. Dissatisfaction among employees is often present, but difficult to isolate. The supervisor should seek to weaken dissatisfaction by keeping promises, being sincere and considerate, keeping employees informed, and so forth.

11. Constructive suggestions should be encouraged during the natural progress of the work.

V. PROCESSES FOR SOLVING PROBLEMS

1. People find their daily tasks more meaningful and satisfying when they can improve them.

2. The causes of problems, or the key factors, are often hidden in the background. Ability to solve problems often involves the ability to isolate them from their backgrounds. There is some substance to the cliché that some persons "can't see the forest for the trees."

3. New procedures are often developed from old ones. Problems should be broken down into manageable parts. New ideas can be adapted from old ones.

4. People think differently in problem-solving situations. Using a logical, patterned approach is often useful. One approach found to be useful includes these steps:
   (a) Define the problem   (d) Weigh and decide
   (b) Establish objectives   (e) Take action
   (c) Get the facts   (f) Evaluate action

VI. TRAINING FOR RESULTS

1. Participants respond best when they feel training is important to them.
2. The supervisor has responsibility for the training and development of those who report to him.
3. When training is delegated to others, great care must be exercised to insure the trainer has knowledge, aptitude, and interest for his work as a trainer.
4. Training (learning) of some type goes on continually. The most successful supervisor makes certain the learning contributes in a productive manner to operational goals.
5. New employees are particularly susceptible to training. Older employees facing new job situations require specific training, as well as having need for development and growth opportunities.
6. Training needs require continuous monitoring.
7. The training officer of an agency is a professional with a responsibility to assist supervisors in solving training problems.
8. Many of the self-development steps important to the supervisor's own growth are equally important to the development of peers and subordinates. Knowledge of these is important when the supervisor consults with others on development and growth opportunities.

VII. HEALTH, SAFETY, AND ACCIDENT PREVENTION

1. Management-minded supervisors take appropriate measures to assist employees in maintaining health and in assuring safe practices in the work environment.
2. Effective safety training and practices help to avoid injury and accidents.
3. Safety should be a management goal. All infractions of safety which are observed should be corrected without exception.
4. Employees' safety attitude, training and instruction, provision of safe tools and equipment, supervision, and leadership are considered highly important factors which contribute to safety and which can be influenced directly by supervisors.
5. When accidents do occur they should be investigated promptly for very important reasons, including the fact that information which is gained can be used to prevent accidents in the future.

VIII. EQUAL EMPLOYMENT OPPORTUNITY

1. The supervisor should endeavor to treat all employees fairly, without regard to religion, race, sex, or national origin.
2. Groups tend to reflect the attitude of the leader. Prejudice can be detected even in very subtle form. Supervisors must strive to create a feeling of mutual respect and confidence in every employee.
3. Complete utilization of all human resources is a national goal. Equitable consideration should be accorded women in the work force, minority-group members, the physically and mentally handicapped, and the older employee. The important question is: "Who can do the job?"
4. Training opportunities, recognition for performance, overtime assignments, promotional opportunities, and all other personnel actions are to be handled on an equitable basis.

13

IX. IMPROVING COMMUNICATIONS

1. Communications is achieving understanding between the sender and the receiver of a message. It also means sharing information -- the creation of understanding.
2. Communication is basic to all human activity. Words are means of conveying meanings; however, real meanings are in people.
3. There are very practical differences in the effectiveness of one-way, impersonal, and two-way communications. Words spoken face-to-face are better understood. Telephone conversations are effective, but lack the rapport of person-to-person exchanges. The whole person communicates.
4. Cooperation and communication in an organization go hand-in-hand. When there is a mutual respect between people, spelling out rules and procedures for communicating is unnecessary.
5. There are several barriers to effective communications. These include failure to listen with respect and understanding, lack of skill in feedback, and misinterpreting the meanings of words used by the speaker. It is also common practice to listen to what we want to hear, and tune out things we do not want to hear.
6. Communication is management's chief problem. The supervisor should accept the challenge to communicate more effectively and to improve interagency and intra-agency communications.
7. The supervisor may often plan for and conduct meetings. The planning phase is critical and may determine the success or the failure of a meeting.
8. Speaking before groups usually requires extra effort. Stage fright may never disappear completely, but it can be controlled.

X. SELF-DEVELOPMENT

1. Every employee is responsible for his own self-development.
2. Toastmaster and toastmistress clubs offer opportunities to improve skills in oral communications.
3. Planning for one's own self-development is of vital importance. Supervisors know their own strengths and limitations better than anyone else.
4. Many opportunities are open to aid the supervisor in his developmental efforts, including job assignments; training opportunities, both governmental and non-governmental -- to include universities and professional conferences and seminars.
5. Programmed instruction offers a means of studying at one's own rate.
6. Where difficulties may arise from a supervisor's being away from his work for training, he may participate in televised home study or correspondence courses to meet his self-development needs.

XI. TEACHING AND TRAINING

A. The Teaching Process

Teaching is encouraging and guiding the learning activities of students toward established goals. In most cases this process consists in five steps: preparation, presentation, summarization, evaluation, and application.

1. Preparation

Preparation is twofold in nature; that of the supervisor and the employee.

Preparation by the supervisor is absolutely essential to success. He must know what, when, where, how, and whom he will teach. Some of the factors that should be considered are:

(1) The objectives   (5) Employee interest
(2) The materials needed   (6) Training aids
(3) The methods to be used (7) Evaluation
(4) Employee participation (8) Summarization

Employee preparation consists in preparing the employee to receive the material. Probably the most important single factor in the preparation of the employee is arousing and maintaining his interest. He must know the objectives of the training, why he is there, how the material can be used, and its importance to him.

2. Presentation

In presentation, have a carefully designed plan and follow it. The plan should be accurate and complete, yet flexible enough to meet situations as they arise. The method of presentation will be determined by the particular situation and objectives.

3. Summary

A summary should be made at the end of every training unit and program. In addition, there may be internal summaries depending on the nature of the material being taught. The important thing is that the trainee must always be able to understand how each part of the new material relates to the whole.

4. Application

The supervisor must arrange work so the employee will be given a chance to apply new knowledge or skills while the material is still clear in his mind and interest is high. The trainee does not really know whether he has learned the material until he has been given a chance to apply it. If the material is not applied, it loses most of its value.

5. Evaluation

The purpose of all training is to promote learning. To determine whether the training has been a success or failure, the supervisor must evaluate this learning.

In the broadest sense evaluation includes all the devices, methods, skills, and techniques used by the supervisor to keep himself and the employees informed as to their progress toward the objectives they are pursuing. The extent to which the employee has mastered the knowledge, skills, and abilities, or changed his attitudes, as determined by the program objectives, is the extent to which instruction has succeeded or failed.

Evaluation should not be confined to the end of the lesson, day, or program but should be used continuously. We shall note later the way this relates to the rest of the teaching process.

B. Teaching Methods

A teaching method is a pattern of identifiable student and instructor activity used in presenting training material.

All supervisors are faced with the problem of deciding which method should be used at a given time.

1. Lecture
     The lecture is direct oral presentation of material by the supervisor. The present trend is to place less emphasis on the trainer's activity and more on that of the trainee.
2. Discussion
     Teaching by discussion or conference involves using questions and other techniques to arouse interest and focus attention upon certain areas, and by doing so creating a learning situation. This can be one of the most valuable methods because it gives the employees an opportunity to express their ideas and pool their knowledge.
3. Demonstration
     The demonstration is used to teach how something works or how to do something. It can be used to show a principle or what the results of a series of actions will be. A well-staged demonstration is particularly effective because it shows proper methods of performance in a realistic manner.
4. Performance
     Performance is one of the most fundamental of all learning techniques or teaching methods. The trainee may be able to tell how a specific operation should be performed but he cannot be sure he knows how to perform the operation until he has done so.

  As with all methods, there are certain advantages and disadvantages to each method.

5. Which Method to Use
     Moreover, there are other methods and techniques of teaching. It is difficult to use any method without other methods entering into it. In any learning situation a combination of methods is usually more effective than any one method alone.

  Finally, evaluation must be integrated into the other aspects of the teaching-learning process.
  It must be used in the motivation of the trainees; it must be used to assist in developing understanding during the training; and it must be related to employee application of the results of training.
  This is distinctly the role of the supervisor.

———

ANSWER SHEET

TEST NO. _____ PART _____ TITLE OF POSITION _____

(AS GIVEN IN EXAMINATION ANNOUNCEMENT - INCLUDE OPTION, IF ANY)

PLACE OF EXAMINATION _____ DATE____ _____

(CITY OR TOWN) (STATE)

RATING

USE THE SPECIAL PENCIL.   MAKE GLOSSY BLACK MARKS.

Make only ONE mark for each answer.   Additional and stray marks may be counted as mistakes.   In making corrections, erase errors COMPLETELY.

ANSWER SHEET

TEST NO. _____ PART _____ TITLE OF POSITION _____

PLACE OF EXAMINATION _____ DATE _____

(CITY OR TOWN)   (STATE)

RATING

USE THE SPECIAL PENCIL. MAKE GLOSSY BLACK MARKS.

	A B C D E		A B C D E		A B C D E		A B C D E		A B C D E
1	⁞⁞ ⁞⁞ ⁞⁞ ⁞⁞ ⁞⁞	26	⁞⁞ ⁞⁞ ⁞⁞ ⁞⁞ ⁞⁞	51	⁞⁞ ⁞⁞ ⁞⁞ ⁞⁞ ⁞⁞	76	⁞⁞ ⁞⁞ ⁞⁞ ⁞⁞ ⁞⁞	101	⁞⁞ ⁞⁞ ⁞⁞ ⁞⁞ ⁞⁞
2	⁞⁞ ⁞⁞ ⁞⁞ ⁞⁞ ⁞⁞	27	⁞⁞ ⁞⁞ ⁞⁞ ⁞⁞ ⁞⁞	52	⁞⁞ ⁞⁞ ⁞⁞ ⁞⁞ ⁞⁞	77	⁞⁞ ⁞⁞ ⁞⁞ ⁞⁞ ⁞⁞	102	⁞⁞ ⁞⁞ ⁞⁞ ⁞⁞ ⁞⁞
3	⁞⁞ ⁞⁞ ⁞⁞ ⁞⁞ ⁞⁞	28	⁞⁞ ⁞⁞ ⁞⁞ ⁞⁞ ⁞⁞	53	⁞⁞ ⁞⁞ ⁞⁞ ⁞⁞ ⁞⁞	78	⁞⁞ ⁞⁞ ⁞⁞ ⁞⁞ ⁞⁞	103	⁞⁞ ⁞⁞ ⁞⁞ ⁞⁞ ⁞⁞
4	⁞⁞ ⁞⁞ ⁞⁞ ⁞⁞ ⁞⁞	29	⁞⁞ ⁞⁞ ⁞⁞ ⁞⁞ ⁞⁞	54	⁞⁞ ⁞⁞ ⁞⁞ ⁞⁞ ⁞⁞	79	⁞⁞ ⁞⁞ ⁞⁞ ⁞⁞ ⁞⁞	104	⁞⁞ ⁞⁞ ⁞⁞ ⁞⁞ ⁞⁞
5	⁞⁞ ⁞⁞ ⁞⁞ ⁞⁞ ⁞⁞	30	⁞⁞ ⁞⁞ ⁞⁞ ⁞⁞ ⁞⁞	55	⁞⁞ ⁞⁞ ⁞⁞ ⁞⁞ ⁞⁞	80	⁞⁞ ⁞⁞ ⁞⁞ ⁞⁞ ⁞⁞	105	⁞⁞ ⁞⁞ ⁞⁞ ⁞⁞ ⁞⁞
6	⁞⁞ ⁞⁞ ⁞⁞ ⁞⁞ ⁞⁞	31	⁞⁞ ⁞⁞ ⁞⁞ ⁞⁞ ⁞⁞	56	⁞⁞ ⁞⁞ ⁞⁞ ⁞⁞ ⁞⁞	81	⁞⁞ ⁞⁞ ⁞⁞ ⁞⁞ ⁞⁞	106	⁞⁞ ⁞⁞ ⁞⁞ ⁞⁞ ⁞⁞
7	⁞⁞ ⁞⁞ ⁞⁞ ⁞⁞ ⁞⁞	32	⁞⁞ ⁞⁞ ⁞⁞ ⁞⁞ ⁞⁞	57	⁞⁞ ⁞⁞ ⁞⁞ ⁞⁞ ⁞⁞	82	⁞⁞ ⁞⁞ ⁞⁞ ⁞⁞ ⁞⁞	107	⁞⁞ ⁞⁞ ⁞⁞ ⁞⁞ ⁞⁞
8	⁞⁞ ⁞⁞ ⁞⁞ ⁞⁞ ⁞⁞	33	⁞⁞ ⁞⁞ ⁞⁞ ⁞⁞ ⁞⁞	58	⁞⁞ ⁞⁞ ⁞⁞ ⁞⁞ ⁞⁞	83	⁞⁞ ⁞⁞ ⁞⁞ ⁞⁞ ⁞⁞	108	⁞⁞ ⁞⁞ ⁞⁞ ⁞⁞ ⁞⁞
9	⁞⁞ ⁞⁞ ⁞⁞ ⁞⁞ ⁞⁞	34	⁞⁞ ⁞⁞ ⁞⁞ ⁞⁞ ⁞⁞	59	⁞⁞ ⁞⁞ ⁞⁞ ⁞⁞ ⁞⁞	84	⁞⁞ ⁞⁞ ⁞⁞ ⁞⁞ ⁞⁞	109	⁞⁞ ⁞⁞ ⁞⁞ ⁞⁞ ⁞⁞
10	⁞⁞ ⁞⁞ ⁞⁞ ⁞⁞ ⁞⁞	35	⁞⁞ ⁞⁞ ⁞⁞ ⁞⁞ ⁞⁞	60	⁞⁞ ⁞⁞ ⁞⁞ ⁞⁞ ⁞⁞	85	⁞⁞ ⁞⁞ ⁞⁞ ⁞⁞ ⁞⁞	110	⁞⁞ ⁞⁞ ⁞⁞ ⁞⁞ ⁞⁞

Make only ONE mark for each answer. Additional and stray marks may be
counted as mistakes. In making corrections, erase errors COMPLETELY.

	A B C D E		A B C D E		A B C D E		A B C D E		A B C D E
11	⁞⁞ ⁞⁞ ⁞⁞ ⁞⁞ ⁞⁞	36	⁞⁞ ⁞⁞ ⁞⁞ ⁞⁞ ⁞⁞	61	⁞⁞ ⁞⁞ ⁞⁞ ⁞⁞ ⁞⁞	86	⁞⁞ ⁞⁞ ⁞⁞ ⁞⁞ ⁞⁞	111	⁞⁞ ⁞⁞ ⁞⁞ ⁞⁞ ⁞⁞
12	⁞⁞ ⁞⁞ ⁞⁞ ⁞⁞ ⁞⁞	37	⁞⁞ ⁞⁞ ⁞⁞ ⁞⁞ ⁞⁞	62	⁞⁞ ⁞⁞ ⁞⁞ ⁞⁞ ⁞⁞	87	⁞⁞ ⁞⁞ ⁞⁞ ⁞⁞ ⁞⁞	112	⁞⁞ ⁞⁞ ⁞⁞ ⁞⁞ ⁞⁞
13	⁞⁞ ⁞⁞ ⁞⁞ ⁞⁞ ⁞⁞	38	⁞⁞ ⁞⁞ ⁞⁞ ⁞⁞ ⁞⁞	63	⁞⁞ ⁞⁞ ⁞⁞ ⁞⁞ ⁞⁞	88	⁞⁞ ⁞⁞ ⁞⁞ ⁞⁞ ⁞⁞	113	⁞⁞ ⁞⁞ ⁞⁞ ⁞⁞ ⁞⁞
14	⁞⁞ ⁞⁞ ⁞⁞ ⁞⁞ ⁞⁞	39	⁞⁞ ⁞⁞ ⁞⁞ ⁞⁞ ⁞⁞	64	⁞⁞ ⁞⁞ ⁞⁞ ⁞⁞ ⁞⁞	89	⁞⁞ ⁞⁞ ⁞⁞ ⁞⁞ ⁞⁞	114	⁞⁞ ⁞⁞ ⁞⁞ ⁞⁞ ⁞⁞
15	⁞⁞ ⁞⁞ ⁞⁞ ⁞⁞ ⁞⁞	40	⁞⁞ ⁞⁞ ⁞⁞ ⁞⁞ ⁞⁞	65	⁞⁞ ⁞⁞ ⁞⁞ ⁞⁞ ⁞⁞	90	⁞⁞ ⁞⁞ ⁞⁞ ⁞⁞ ⁞⁞	115	⁞⁞ ⁞⁞ ⁞⁞ ⁞⁞ ⁞⁞
16	⁞⁞ ⁞⁞ ⁞⁞ ⁞⁞ ⁞⁞	41	⁞⁞ ⁞⁞ ⁞⁞ ⁞⁞ ⁞⁞	66	⁞⁞ ⁞⁞ ⁞⁞ ⁞⁞ ⁞⁞	91	⁞⁞ ⁞⁞ ⁞⁞ ⁞⁞ ⁞⁞	116	⁞⁞ ⁞⁞ ⁞⁞ ⁞⁞ ⁞⁞
17	⁞⁞ ⁞⁞ ⁞⁞ ⁞⁞ ⁞⁞	42	⁞⁞ ⁞⁞ ⁞⁞ ⁞⁞ ⁞⁞	67	⁞⁞ ⁞⁞ ⁞⁞ ⁞⁞ ⁞⁞	92	⁞⁞ ⁞⁞ ⁞⁞ ⁞⁞ ⁞⁞	117	⁞⁞ ⁞⁞ ⁞⁞ ⁞⁞ ⁞⁞
18	⁞⁞ ⁞⁞ ⁞⁞ ⁞⁞ ⁞⁞	43	⁞⁞ ⁞⁞ ⁞⁞ ⁞⁞ ⁞⁞	68	⁞⁞ ⁞⁞ ⁞⁞ ⁞⁞ ⁞⁞	93	⁞⁞ ⁞⁞ ⁞⁞ ⁞⁞ ⁞⁞	118	⁞⁞ ⁞⁞ ⁞⁞ ⁞⁞ ⁞⁞
19	⁞⁞ ⁞⁞ ⁞⁞ ⁞⁞ ⁞⁞	44	⁞⁞ ⁞⁞ ⁞⁞ ⁞⁞ ⁞⁞	69	⁞⁞ ⁞⁞ ⁞⁞ ⁞⁞ ⁞⁞	94	⁞⁞ ⁞⁞ ⁞⁞ ⁞⁞ ⁞⁞	119	⁞⁞ ⁞⁞ ⁞⁞ ⁞⁞ ⁞⁞
20	⁞⁞ ⁞⁞ ⁞⁞ ⁞⁞ ⁞⁞	45	⁞⁞ ⁞⁞ ⁞⁞ ⁞⁞ ⁞⁞	70	⁞⁞ ⁞⁞ ⁞⁞ ⁞⁞ ⁞⁞	95	⁞⁞ ⁞⁞ ⁞⁞ ⁞⁞ ⁞⁞	120	⁞⁞ ⁞⁞ ⁞⁞ ⁞⁞ ⁞⁞
21	⁞⁞ ⁞⁞ ⁞⁞ ⁞⁞ ⁞⁞	46	⁞⁞ ⁞⁞ ⁞⁞ ⁞⁞ ⁞⁞	71	⁞⁞ ⁞⁞ ⁞⁞ ⁞⁞ ⁞⁞	96	⁞⁞ ⁞⁞ ⁞⁞ ⁞⁞ ⁞⁞	121	⁞⁞ ⁞⁞ ⁞⁞ ⁞⁞ ⁞⁞
22	⁞⁞ ⁞⁞ ⁞⁞ ⁞⁞ ⁞⁞	47	⁞⁞ ⁞⁞ ⁞⁞ ⁞⁞ ⁞⁞	72	⁞⁞ ⁞⁞ ⁞⁞ ⁞⁞ ⁞⁞	97	⁞⁞ ⁞⁞ ⁞⁞ ⁞⁞ ⁞⁞	122	⁞⁞ ⁞⁞ ⁞⁞ ⁞⁞ ⁞⁞
23	⁞⁞ ⁞⁞ ⁞⁞ ⁞⁞ ⁞⁞	48	⁞⁞ ⁞⁞ ⁞⁞ ⁞⁞ ⁞⁞	73	⁞⁞ ⁞⁞ ⁞⁞ ⁞⁞ ⁞⁞	98	⁞⁞ ⁞⁞ ⁞⁞ ⁞⁞ ⁞⁞	123	⁞⁞ ⁞⁞ ⁞⁞ ⁞⁞ ⁞⁞
24	⁞⁞ ⁞⁞ ⁞⁞ ⁞⁞ ⁞⁞	49	⁞⁞ ⁞⁞ ⁞⁞ ⁞⁞ ⁞⁞	74	⁞⁞ ⁞⁞ ⁞⁞ ⁞⁞ ⁞⁞	99	⁞⁞ ⁞⁞ ⁞⁞ ⁞⁞ ⁞⁞	124	⁞⁞ ⁞⁞ ⁞⁞ ⁞⁞ ⁞⁞
25	⁞⁞ ⁞⁞ ⁞⁞ ⁞⁞ ⁞⁞	50	⁞⁞ ⁞⁞ ⁞⁞ ⁞⁞ ⁞⁞	75	⁞⁞ ⁞⁞ ⁞⁞ ⁞⁞ ⁞⁞	100	⁞⁞ ⁞⁞ ⁞⁞ ⁞⁞ ⁞⁞	125	⁞⁞ ⁞⁞ ⁞⁞ ⁞⁞ ⁞